I am Micky

I AM MICKY

I am Micky

"For we are God's handiwork, created in Christ Jesus to do good works, which God prepared in advance for us to do."

Ephesians 2:10 NIV

Micky Maris

I AM MICKY

I am Micky

First Printing, 2024

Micky Maris

Altenburg

https://linktr.ee/iammicky

DEDICATION

I dedicate this book to all those who gave me a chance when I needed it—friends and strangers whose encouragement, kindness, and belief in me shaped my journey. Your support has been a guiding light during challenging times, and I am forever grateful for your presence in my life.

I AM MICKY

I AM MICKY

CONTENTS

I AM MICKY

About The Author

I am Micky Maris Obadiaru, born in 1995 into the family of Mr. and Mrs. Obadiaru. I grew up in a chaotic household with three brothers and a sister. After studying Home Economics Management & Education at the University of Benin, Edo State, I pursued my passion for Quality Management, earning a Master's from the University of Kassel and Hochschule Fulda, Germany. Focusing on Quality Management in the food industry, I currently work as a Quality Manager in the dairy industry.

I draw inspiration from many individuals, including Linda Ikeji, whose entrepreneurial spirit motivates me; Viola Davis, an American actress whose talent and resilience inspire me; Ifedayo Agoro of Dang Lifestyle and my first boss, whose mentorship shaped my professional journey.

My philosophy revolves around believing that *"every small act of kindness has the power to make a big difference."* With these values at heart, I am committed to empowering individuals and communities to thrive by providing resources and support to help them advance.

In my leisure time, I like to cook, listen to music, play table tennis, explore the latest techno-logical trends, invest, and volunteer in my community.

Looking forward, I aim to pursue a career as a **Food Auditor, launch a food safety app,** and engage in **German politics.** Additionally, I am dedicated to expanding the impact of my **NGO - The Micky Maris Foundation,** volunteering initiatives, and coaching programs—focusing on helping individuals secure job opportunities and make informed investment decisions.

PREFACE

In recent years, attention has increasingly focused on the subtle pandemic of domestic violence, particularly its effects on innocent children. As we explore this profound issue, we must confront its realities and acknowledge its widespread impact on vulnerable members of society.

According to a report by *Deutsche Welle (2023),* in the last three years, **Germany** has seen a worrying increase in reports of domestic violence, highlighting the urgency to address this serious issue. Factors like economic stress, substance abuse, and cultural views on gender play a significant role in this rise of domestic violence. Also, lockdowns due to the pandemic made the situation worse, leading to more reports of abuse in homes.

At the same time, these cases keep happening in **Nigeria** at an alarming rate, showing the harsh realities countless individuals face behind closed doors. These numbers serve as a reminder to us that we urgently need to work together and speak up to break the cycle of abuse and help those who are suffering.

Amidst these scary statistics lay the personal journey of an individual who navigated through the rough landscape of domestic violence, emerging as a source of hope and resilience to others.

As the author of this book, I share with you a private glimpse at my personal life. This life endured loneliness and despair without family support. In my darkest moments, I discovered and found solace in a higher power, a divine presence that guided me through challenges and gave me the strength to keep going.

Through the pages of this book, I implore you to join me on an extraordinary journey where faith in God becomes the cornerstone of healing and redemption. I share real-life stories of talking with God—times when prayers went beyond what we could touch and became real solutions to problems, showing us the path to healing and restoration.

Today, the scars of the past do not hold me back. Instead, I feel stronger because I have overcome tough times through the triumph of my spirit. With profound gratitude, I extend my hand to share my story of survival and the roadmap to succeeding in a harsh world.

With each chapter, I have shared many practical and valuable lessons from my experience to help you navigate life's challenges and become victorious.

This book is a glimmer of light in the darkness, showing us hope, healing, and renewal. May it serve as proof that people have the power to overcome difficult times, inspiring others who dream of a brighter tomorrow.

I AM MICKY

I AM MICKY

CONTENT WARNING

This book contains the subject matter of domestic violence, mental health, and racism.

I AM MICKY

I am Micky

I AM MICKY

CHAPTER ONE

EARLY CHILDHOOD

REFLECTING ON MY early childhood, I realized that most people recall precise memories of  what they did, how they felt, and the company they kept during their growing-up years. However, I am an exception, as I only recall a little from the past. A glance at my early years came from my elder brother, whom I will call P. I remember him recounting a rough incident when I was around three or four years old; the details are sketchy. He told me that I fought with another child while playing with sand. The child took something that belonged to me, and when I tried everything possible to retrieve it, he was adamant.

1

I AM MICKY

We started arguing, and somehow, a small stone found its way into my hand in the heat of the argument. In anger, I used it to hit the child on the head, and it resulted in an unexpected injury. Ouch! Was it Micky, me, who did that? I still find this hard to believe. Perhaps so.

I was born into the Obadiaru family, hailing from the ancient city of **Benin,** which is famous for its rich history in bronze artistry.  However, as evidenced by my passport, I was born in **Sapele, Delta State.** My husband humorously refers to **Sapele** as *"Sapbele"* with his unique **German** accent. **Sapele** is a primary town in **Delta State** that is not far from the great city of **Benin.** It is a hub for **Nigeria's** timber industry as its sawmills buzz with activities, echoing the city's dynamic spirit.

2

Interestingly, **Sapele** is also renowned for its indigenous beverage, *sapele water (ogogoro or kai kai)*. Legend has it that most **Sapele** natives taste this concentrated mixture at a tender age. As my childhood memory draws blank, I can't confirm whether I indulged in drinking it or not as a child.

The Movement – Sapele to Benin City

Frequent moves marked my growing-up life as my father's profession made way for my family's migrating tendencies. When I was five, we bid farewell to **Sapele** and relocated to **Benin City.** As a successful engineer, my father's skills were in high demand. With a **diploma** from a **Technical College** in **Delta State,** he embarked on a thriving career, which united him with the government on massive projects. While my father expanded his career and continued his big government projects, my mother, like most women, had no chance to attend school. During her time, most African women were only allowed to learn trades or go to the farm, then become homemakers and bear children for their husbands.

"When there is an increase in a man's finances, there comes the attitude. No, I'm not generalizing; I'm talking about my father. You may be lucky to have a different father."

My Mother's Struggle in Silence

My father was a serial adulterer. He went about engaging in extramarital affairs with different women in **Benin City,** leaving my mum mostly alone at home to take care of four children. Not only was he a serial adulterer, he was also a woman beater. I didn't fully understand the extent of his behavior until I was around seven years old. My mother barely smiled or laughed as she was always in a sorrowful state, with news of my father's philandering lifestyle always getting to her.

Sometimes, we had house helpers, but it did not make anything manageable for my mum, who always tried to keep herself busy, all in a bid to pay less attention to her husband's lifestyle. Looking back, I realize why my brain refused to assimilate many early childhood memories. Perhaps they were too painful to remember. If those memories had stayed with me, I would have been even more traumatized than I already was.

At just seven years old, I remember an incident that would have landed my mother in jail. It was a hectic day when my mother, tired of enduring my father's betrayals, decided to take the laws into her own hands. She heard from a reliable source that his secretary, with whom he was having an affair at their company, was coming to our house to deliver a package.

Determined to confront her, my mother woke up early and prepared herself. She cleaned the house thoroughly and washed the dirty clothes while arming herself with a pestle *(a weighty tool with a round end used for grinding substances like spices),* waiting for the secretary. We could see the bloodshot anger in her eyes. *"I am going to break this woman's head today,"* she said. For a quick moment, the possibility of violence and death hung in the air.

The secretary finally arrived, and my mother argued with her, demanding to know what she was doing in our house. My mother's rage and sorrow reached a boiling point. But somehow, she controlled herself, sparing us all the consequences of my father's actions. Phew! Now imagine she did, and I saw someone's brain all over the place at age seven.

Reflecting on that moment now, I realize the depth of pain and betrayal that my mother endured and the strength she showed in the face of it, all because my father could not be faithful to a woman he married and promised to love and protect.

My Mother's Struggle Through Navigating Faith, Fear and Oppression

My mother deeply loved God, as He was the only person she could talk to. However, she did not have a chance to serve him as she desired due to the oppressive control of my father. This action took a toll on her health and well-being, subjecting her to physical, mental, and emotional abuse that left her getting sick more often than usual. Adding to her struggles, my father's family showed her little or no kindness, and her own family could not do anything as they feared my father too much to intervene in the situation.

My siblings and I rarely had a relationship with our grandparents; any semblance of one was almost non-existent. For example, I never met my maternal grandmother until I was 13. Unlike many children in **Europe** who enjoy close bonds with their amazing grandparents, I had no such connection to any of mine. While **European** grandparents often step in to compensate for any parental shortcomings, I missed out on this kind of relationship.

With my paternal grandmother, I met her early enough. However, she instilled fear in me due to her association with native practices as a native doctor. Rumors had it that she had seven husbands and many children. The stories my mother told me about her added to my unease. Whenever she visited my father, she usually carried fetish and ugly items for her enchantments. Once, when she visited our home, she came with a tortoise, leaving me disturbed and scared. This lingering fear of my grandmother's practice kept me distanced from older people for years, reluctant to even be near them, let alone embrace them, due to fear of the unknown.

A Lesson on Empathy and Taking Responsibilities for One's Actions

Intelligence runs in our family—all my siblings are incredibly talented and brilliant, and we inherited these traits from both parents. Despite growing up in an abusive household, we always strived to excel in school and bring good grades back home. My father and mother prioritized education by ensuring we had home teachers who came to teach us for extra hours; *education is vital as a guiding principle in life.*

We usually didn't get lunch for school, as I don't remember my mum ever packing one for us due to stress and her health issues—she was mainly in the house of God, seeking solutions from him for her health and her falling marriage. One particular incident stood out for me in my memory. That day, I arrived at school hungry, without snacks or money, and did not know what to do. Usually, at noon, teachers call out the names of students whose parents had paid for their snacks. We had two people named Maris in my class, as that was my first name in the past, although presently, most people know me as Micky. I will describe how the name *"Micky"* came into the picture.

During lunchtime, the teacher called, *"Maris, come for your lunch."* I assumed she was referring to me. Hurriedly, I approached her and eagerly accepted the snack before she changed her mind. My mum always told us about manna falling from heaven, so I thought this could be one of Jesus's many miracles; he saw me hungry and then made the teacher call my name. I ate the snack, feeling like it was one of the mysteries of life, as this had never happened before.

However, my joy was short-lived when the teacher realized she had made a mistake. The snack was for the other pupil, Maris, and I had no idea. My teacher angrily said, *"It wasn't your lunch to eat Maris. You ate the lunch of your classmate."* I was shocked and embarrassed. The other Maris began to cry, and I started crying too. At that young age, I realized how it felt to have what was yours taken away from you and given to another person. It was a sad moment for me and the poor little Maris.

Guilt flooded my thoughts, and I wondered, *"Was this stealing?"* I did not know what else to do to soothe her as I had already eaten and digested the snack, but this made me decide to be more careful. Going forward, I never wanted to bring tears to other people's eyes, as this experience taught me an important lesson on empathy and the consequences of one's actions.

I AM MICKY

The Award

The following year, I graduated from class two to class three. I received an award for being the best student and another award whose purpose I can't recall. My father dropped me off at school the morning of my prize-giving before heading to a

 meeting. Before the drop-off, I was feeling sick. Why? I hated riding in his car because of the distinct scented perfume he had in it, a characteristic of his Peugeot 504. He loved his car and the scent so much, but the smell made me sick whenever he drove me to school. Only that, on this particular day, I was sicker than usual, and I wasn't in the best mood for anything.

During the prize-giving ceremony, they handed me a scroll. I was so curious to open it and see what was inside, but I couldn't, as it seemed complicated. Seeing that my mother and father did

not make it to the occasion, I decided to try and open it with the only trick I knew, which was to use my teeth to remove the cover of the scroll. In the process, I broke something. Phew! I broke my teeth. Yes, you get that for being a strong, independent woman too early in life—breaking your teeth.

A Hustle for Lunch Money

After the lunch incident at school, where I mistakenly ate another child's snack, I became more careful and serious about ensuring I had something to eat for lunch so I wouldn't go hungry again. This time, I developed a strange skill of taking money from my mother's purse as she didn't give me any then. She wasn't working because she relied on my father, the same person who shut down her business. She used to own a salon, which he stopped her from operating and prevented her from pursuing other business ventures. My father further converted her hairdryers into incubators *(machines for hatching eggs)*. Quite creative, isn't it? Oh! The extent he went to make her a stay-at-home mum and a dependent wife.

My mother had a brown purse filled with mostly shiny notes. She mainly obtained these notes from the feeding money my father gave her. These notes were in various denominations, consisting of ten (10) or five (5) naira. She often used these notes to give offerings to God in church. Given the dilemma I faced in school due to lack of lunch money, I told myself I was God's child and deserved a piece of the pie.

Every night before bed, I would take my mother's brown purse from her room and throw it under the chair in the living room, as this was the part of the house where I slept, as I didn't have a private room as a child. In the morning, I would sneakingly retrieve the purse from under the chair and take a note of either five (0.0041 euros) or ten (0.0082 euros) Naira as my lunch money for the day. I convinced myself I was taking a piece of God's food and not stealing, but in my conscience, I knew it was stealing.

Single Parenthood with Unwavering Strength and Determination

In 2003, tragedy struck as my paternal grandmother fell ill and eventually passed away. I vividly recall the events surrounding her death, as my mother was heavily pregnant at that time. My sister and I accompanied her to shop for baby items at the market. We saw her struggle throughout the shopping trip, her burden evident in every step she took as she was close to her delivery date. While shopping, I believe her water broke, and she had to make an urgent call to my father. Amidst this confusion, my father hurriedly took her to the hospital, where she had my baby brother. He entered the world in February; two months later, my father's mother died.

Despite the arrival of a new child and the loss of his mother, my father was making preparations to leave **Nigeria** and relocate to **Germany**. He was determined to leave **Nigeria**. Considering he had many issues with the government and business partners, it was his only way out of the waters as his business was beginning to fail. At some point, he faced a lawsuit in court. My mother did advise him to settle the disputes amicably out of court, but he didn't listen. In the long run, he lost everything he had worked for, which took him a long time to achieve, and ended up with so much debt. *"Well, he never listens to his wife."*

He was to choose between participating in his mother's burial preparations or traveling to save himself from being broke. Well, he did decide to travel and left my mother with four young children and a newborn child without any financial or family support. *"How thoughtful of him!"*

My mother faced the challenge of single-handedly caring for four young children and a newborn. She juggled the responsibilities of bathing, feeding, and caring for the newborn, all while attending to the needs of the rest of us and managing the household. It was one of the most challenging chapters in my mother's life as she courageously navigated the trials of single parenthood with determined strength and perseverance.

We didn't hear from my father three months after he had successfully arrived in **Germany.** However, his absence during this period brought a sense of peace as my mother cried less and had fewer bruises. Our living conditions changed, and my mother started giving us lunch money or lunch, which showed that she would have been generous before, but she had no means.

How Domestic Violence Affects a Child's Life

We had a house help before my father traveled, but my mother sent her away. She physically abused us, feeding us the food we hated most (maybe this was why I developed so many food intolerances) and hitting us with a belt. How happy I was when she left.

Unfortunately, physical punishment is common in many African households, and I wouldn't say I liked it. For instance, the house help mistreated my elder brothers severely, using them as tables to eat or as stools to rest her legs. If they resisted, she would beat them or lock them away in the kitchen.

Also, I was occasionally locked up, but not as frequently as my brothers. It's sad to know that my mother was not aware of these abuses, as we were afraid to speak up, fearing blame or further punishment. When both abusive figures left—my father to Germany and our help back to her parents, it was a relief.

In my early childhood, I would say both parents lacked essential parental skills for a child's growth and development. There were no bedtime stories from my dad, no kisses, no hugs, and no words of encouragement—just gifts and food. While my dad was financially supportive, providing for school fees and educational needs, he was emotionally and physically distant from our lives. Meanwhile, my mum was physically present but emotionally distant.

A study conducted by **Vu, N.L. et al. (2016)** explored how children's mental health is affected over time by witnessing violence between intimate partners. They found that being exposed to such violence during childhood can cause problems like anxiety, depression, and PTSD later in life. The study stresses the need for early help and support for kids who witness domestic violence to reduce the risk of lasting mental health issues.

CHAPTER TWO

THE FIRST CALL/RETURN

ONE FATEFUL DAY, a knock at our door interrupted our routine. Our neighbor delivered a message: *"We just got a call from your father. Please inform your mother and siblings that he will call again. Be at my house in 30 minutes."* We all dressed hurriedly and went to the neighbor's house, unsure how to feel about this unexpected call. I was relieved that he was alive and that maybe my mother would be happy to know that her husband was not dead. This man has done nothing but harm her mentally and physically. If I were in her shoes, I would be traumatized to take the call.

When the call came in, we each took our turn to speak to him, although my youngest brother was too young to understand or respond. For him, our father was but a distant figure, absent for the first three years of his life. *"Yes! My dad had never visited **Nigeria** during those three years."* He stayed in **Europe** but instructed his friend to visit us occasionally. Due to the constant visits, my baby brother thought he was his father. Although my father was not present physically, he occasionally sent gifts: shoes, clothes, and money to support us, but those gifts could never fill the void left by his absence. After that call, I can't remember my feelings, but I was relieved that my father was alive and well.

My mother's mental and physical health continually deteriorated as she navigated the challenges of single parenthood. She prayed more and more frequently and sometimes was up late at night, seeking the face of God. She cut our hair at some point due to insufficient time to make it in the day. All these sad events were painful, but I was hopeful; I was always a promising child.

The constant inflow of cash and gifts, a peaceful environment, and no fights and abuses slowly improved our situation. My mother started to add weight and looked more beautiful. She wasn't getting sick as frequently as before. I guess she finally realized she had to move on with her life.

The Origin of Micky

My name, Micky, started as a joke. It originated from a childhood encounter with a pair of shoes my father sent me from **Italy** (he relocated from **Germany** to **Italy**), which I wore to school. At school, a young boy named Destiny saw my pair of shoes and said, *"Those are Mickey Mouse shoes."* I responded, *"No, it is not. They are mine".* Then he asked, *"So you are Micky"?* And I answered, *"Yes, I am MICKY."* Everyone laughed as Destiny and a few other students teased me, but I wasn't bothered as I would always do a funny dance in return for my excitement of wearing a new shoe and my love for Mickey Mouse.

When I shared this funny experience with my father during his call later in the day, he embraced the name, and it stuck. That is how I got the name Micky, of Hebrew origin, with an interpretation of *Who resembles God?* Officially, I added it to all my certificates at age 16.

The Return of My Father

In 2007, a peculiar incident preceded my father's return from **Italy**. I was outside on our front porch when I witnessed two doves alight upon our flat, and they both flew away, an omen of what was to come. The next day, my father returned from **Italy**. His return brought mixed emotions: joy at his homecoming and fear of the disruption of peace it might bring. My baby brother was seeing our father for the first time in three years. He called him uncle instead of father because he never knew him. Emotionally, my baby brother suffered the most growing up without his father. Perhaps it was for the best that he didn't get to see who his father truly was at a young age.

Rhetorically, I asked myself: Is he a changed man now? Will our situation be better? Will my mother get beaten again? Sadly, the following weeks revealed the truth—his return began another trouble. The night my father returned, he complained that he didn't get a proper welcome meal. My mother gave him oatmeal instead of the pounded yam he wanted, as that was what was available, as she had no idea he would be returning to **Nigeria** at that time. I was shocked when this argument escalated into a family meeting.

Moving into a New Environment

When my father was away in **Europe** for three years, he entrusted my mother with a house project, which she supervised and built faithfully with her blood and sweat. One morning, my father woke up and said to my mother, *"The family will have to move to the new house in **Evobomodu**."* My mother, astonished, opposed him, saying, *"The house is not completed yet, and these children will miss their school friends. I think it might not be the right time to move"*. Instantly, my father disagreed with her decision. *"Most African men never listen to their* *wives. Yes, I am generalizing now.*" Despite my mother's opposition, considering it was still an unfinished project, my father insisted on relocating us to the new house.

I started secondary school early because I received a double promotion from class 5 to class 6. I attended the **Conite Group of Schools, Benin City,** while my elder siblings attended a different school. At **Conite,** I made my first best friend, Chelsea, whom I remember fondly. Her parents, who owned the school, were also pastors. Chelsea was a fantastic friend, and we planned to remain friends as we grew older, but this plan was caught short due to unforeseen circumstances.

Over the next few weeks, we started to pack our belongings. I was about to move far away from my best friend and school. I never saw her again, up to this day. When we got to the new house and settled in, we became lonelier and cried more often. My father noticed this and offered we could call our friends, which we did, but this didn't change much, considering it was a new environment. This situation yet again proved that my mother was right. The move was disruptive, severing ties with friends and uprooting our lives.

The Dreadful Attack

Introducing my siblings—Prince, Preston, Joyce, and Jemie. My big brother, Prince, is four years older than I am. The second, Preston, is two years older than I am, but he is not my biggest fan. There is Joyce, my only sister, and my baby brother Jemie. We are a squad of five, and I am the middle child. We faced the challenges of our rough upbringing together.

In our new community, my father started to make new friends and business contacts. He talked mainly about his time in **Italy,** which brought us so much attention, but not all was positive.

One night, we heard loud sounds from our parents' room and became awake. We thought it was a fight between our parents again, only to realize it was an invasion by armed robbers. Amidst the confusion about how they got in, my father was begging them not to shoot him.

My elder brother, Prince, who tends to be the brave one, came out of the room and tried to challenge the armed robbers, but my father stopped him and pleaded with them not to attack his son. He pleaded for our safety, surrendering his possessions to protect his family. They quickly took what they could and left hurriedly.

We called the police, but as most **Nigerians** know, they never show up on time. This incident left us shaken and vulnerable, with little hope of justice from the authorities. With my father's gold and money gone, he was back to having nothing. His passport was safe, but his dream of returning to **Italy** was dashed with no money. Instead, he embarked on a new business venture.

Adjusting to our New Environment

We started a new school, and this time, we all went to the same school called **Unity Group of School**. My siblings and I adjusted as we found solace in each other's company. I loved being in school because it sharpened my ability to study harder. At school, I was a member of the girls' football team. Football was my passion and a way to escape my reality at home. I wanted to play football professionally, but I had no support from my family.

Finishing secondary school was a struggle because our father could not pay our school fees on time. My siblings and I always begged the principal not to send us home from school for owing. It was always a shameful and embracing experience. We were top students, yet our academic pursuits were marred by financial instability.

Our father's business struggles always left us begging. He had no savings for the rainy day, which made us all suffer the consequences, especially my mother. He would beat her at the sightless provocation. I longed to defend my mother from my father's abuse but lacked the courage to intervene as I was still young. As tensions continued to mount at home, my elder brother, Prince, started to fight back, signaling a turning point in our family dynamics.

Life Before University and a Mother's Trial

Every day, I wished I could escape the constant drama around me, but my only hope was to go to the university. At age 14, I took the **West African Examination Council (WAEC) Examination**. My elder brother, Preston, and I were not supposed to write this examination as our father couldn't afford the fee. As

usual, we begged the principal and teachers and convinced them we could pay before the exams started. The principal allowed us to write the exams as we were one of his best students, and luckily, my father came up with the money. He sent it to us two days before the final papers, and we paid, although he called back the next day to say he wanted the money for a quick business. We were lucky because the school has a non-refundable policy.

Writing that exam brought me one step closer to my freedom. The wishes I usually had to disappear from home started at age 12. I would lock myself in my father's room when he was at work and daydream about my life if I finally left the house. Only that I felt it would be a betrayal to my younger siblings. So, I promised myself I would also make an escape route for them when I became successful.

One day, my father severely beat my mother over the food she prepared because he didn't like it. She got angry and ran away. Despite our frantic search, we couldn't find her. My father decided to care for us for the next few days of her absence. That was the first time I ever saw my dad cook. He made equsi soup, and it was delicious. *"It was funny how my dad could cook, yet he never deemed it fit to assist my mother."*

Desperate to find my mom, he contacted her family members, pleading for information on her whereabouts. My father's uncle managed to contact her and convinced her to return, citing the welfare of her children. *"Typical of African family members and churches. They would see you in a crisis and ask you to return to it."* I missed her, but I thought it was best that she was safe somewhere else (there was no safety and defense for her anywhere, from the society and the church). Despite her coming back, the beating didn't stop.

While waiting for my WAEC result, I occupied my time to learn something productive. I was 15 years old at that time. Upon a schoolmate's recommendation, I enrolled in a skills center to learn computer and secretarial studies free of charge for six months. It was a free project by the **Edo State Women Affair & Social Development.** The skills I

acquired here helped me later in life and are still helpful to me today. Meanwhile, my dad relocated to **Delta State** to launch his company.

A Journey to a New Beginning

On this fateful day, I received the long-awaited good news: The WAEC results were finally out, and I could check them. With eager expectation, I hurried to the nearest business center with some friends. As I checked my results, relief flooded over me—I had passed! Bursting with joy and a broad smile, I descended the stairs. Then, a man in the business center observed me, approached me, remarked on my behavior, and expressed interest in hiring me. He asked if I needed a job, and I answered yes, but I was only open to working part-time because I still had to complete my training in the skills center. Since the training was free, I needed to get through, learn well, and get certified. He agreed that I should work part-time, which was how I got my first job. That marked the beginning of my experience.

"Focusing on money without looking for a skill is a path bent to failure. Hence, it was my idea to do both the training and the work part-time."

At the shop, I sold Compact Discs (CDs) and earned 5000 (4.12 euro) naira monthly. I bought my first phone and occasionally supported my mother with that money. Upon passing the WAEC exam, it was time to write the **Joint Admission Matriculation Board (JAMB) Examination.** I was excited to share the news with my father, so I called him, only to receive unexpected advice. He congratulated me on my WAEC success but suggested I wait before pursuing a university education, citing that I was too young and needed my elder brothers to get in first. However, I refused.

I AM MICKY

Determined to forge my path, I sold my phone—the one I had purchased with my hard-earned salary to fund the purchase of the JAMB form. I combined learning a skill, working, and intensively studying for the examination.

As I said earlier, my elder brother, Preston, is not my biggest fan. That way, we didn't communicate much about our plans and visions. I believed he harbored resentment towards me because I did better than him at school, coupled with the comparisons made by our peers who bullied him constantly with the fact that his baby sister outperformed him academically. My parents also made it more complicated by giving me preferential treatment. Undeterred by family conflict, I made plans alone to go to the university even though my brother and I had left secondary school together.

I continued preparing for the JAMB exam all by myself, keeping my plans from my mother to spare her the worry. I went for the exam alone, without family members, accompanied by my schoolmate and her boyfriend, who was writing in the same center. After sitting for the exam, I waited for the results anxiously. After a few weeks, the result came out, and I passed with a score of **216.** Excitedly, I shared the news with my father: *"Hey, Father, I sold my phone, took the JAMB exam, and passed."* His response was encouraging, *"Wow! I am so proud of you. I knew you would do it."* Yet, amidst his praises, I couldn't shake the thought: *"Did he genuinely believe in me? Did he understand the sacrifices I made to achieve this?"*

The University Pursuit

After JAMB, there was the **post-Unified Tertiary Matriculation Examination (UTME),** another crucial university-acceptance exam. My father covered the fees, and thankfully, I passed. With my skills training nearly complete, I anxiously awaited university admission (**the University of Benin** was my dream university)**,** my sole ticket to freedom. The wait felt endless. I hoped for admission. For the record, I wanted to study **Medicine** or

Microbiology as I loved science but wasn't a big fan of Chemistry.

Remember the job I mentioned? *"Oh, yeah! I was a hustler."* One exhausting evening after work, I returned home feeling tired and stressed. Despite the tiredness, I logged into the university portal using my phone to check if I was offered admission. To my amazement, the message read, ***"Congratulations, you have been offered admission to study Home Economics Management & Education."*** I vividly recall that moment—it felt like a ticket to heaven. Excited, I rushed to my mother's room to share the news. While she was happy, our reasons for joy differed. Although I didn't get the course I initially desired, this was the escape I needed. Whether I studied **Botany** or **Zoology** didn't matter; what mattered was leaving that hell of a home behind to attend the great University of Benin. This change would benefit me later in life while shaping my future.

I AM MICKY

I wasted no time informing my father. *"Please, sir, you need to raise money because I am going to university."* I immediately began making plans, reaching out to others who attended the same university. Through this effort, I connected with two amazing ladies, one of whom later offered me a place to stay at the university.

I got the money I needed from my father for the acceptance and school fees. Accompanied by my mother, we headed to the university with my bags and belongings this time. I planned to stay with a woman named Val, whom I had met online on Facebook. Despite my mom's skepticism about staying with a stranger, we proceeded with this option, as it was the only one available. Val graciously welcomed me into her home, allowing me to stay free of charge while I searched for a hostel.

Unforeseen Twist: The Shock of My Life

The following day, I had to pay my acceptance fee at the university. Little did I know, this marked my first mistake. I paid the acceptance fee to the school account and started attending classes. It was there that I met Charity. Unknown to us, we had both made the same error, a realization that would come to light in the following weeks.

One day, to our surprise, the school clearance officer informed us that we couldn't complete the university entry clearance. Confused, we sought clarification from him. To our astonishment, he told us that this campus was not the right one for us. I couldn't help but wonder if there were two universities of Benin in Benin, Edo State.

Determined to rectify the mistake, Charity and I proceeded to the Bursary department. However, what awaited us there left us utterly stunned. It turned out that the prestigious **University of Benin** had recently partnered with another institution in **Asaba,**

Delta State, to establish a new campus—and we were students of this new campus. The audacity they had to execute this without informing us was beyond belief.

We were desperate for solutions and didn't dwell on the problem. We focused on getting our

money refunded so we could pay for the new campus in Asaba. We asked the man, *"How can we get our money refunded so we can go to the new campus and pay there"*? The man realized all this was new to us.

I could cry that day, but something unexpected happened. As the clearance officer scanned my name on the computer, he recognized my surname and asked, *"Are you related to the Obadiaru family?"* I responded affirmatively, joyfully, *"Yes, I am."* Perhaps he knew my father, I thought. To my amazement, he revealed, *"I know your uncle, the chief—the Obadiaru of* **Benin kingdom.**" My father is from a royal family, and this connection seemed to work in my favor. *"Wonderful!"* he exclaimed. *"I will be of great assistance to you in resolving this issue.* Write *a letter and submit it to the Bursar's office, then return tomorrow."* True to his word, we returned the next day, and he had successfully resolved the matter, securing our refund. *"That was the first and last time my father's surname worked like magic for me."*

As I prepared for my journey to a new state and campus, a wave of panic washed over me. Leaving **Benin** meant being far away from my siblings. *"How would they cope with the distance, I wondered?"* Despite my concerns, I forged ahead, marking the second time I found myself redirected— first with a different course than I had intended to study, and now with a different campus in **Asaba.**

CHAPTER THREE

UNIVERSITY STUDENT LIFE

ASABA, LOCATED ON the banks of **River Niger** in **Delta State, Nigeria,** is a vibrant city blending rich history with modern life. Its diverse culture and bustling urban scene make it an exciting destination for travelers seeking a taste of tradition and contemporary living. Even though I was new there, it felt like home to me, considering I was born in this state. That way, I felt welcomed.

I was super excited to be the first person in my family to attend the university. I was proud of myself. My elder brother, Prince, had to join my father at his company in **Delta State.** Our father gave him money to buy a **JAMB** form when I was still in secondary school. Unfortunately, he squandered the money, didn't register for the exam, and missed the opportunity to attend university. My immediate elder brother, Preston, followed the same direction despite both of them completing secondary school. Their paths divided from the academic route, leading them to find employment in our father's company. Meanwhile, I continued my journey through higher education, inspired by their experiences to seize every opportunity before me.

I left Charity in **Benin City** as she needed more time to sort herself out before resuming. A week later, she came to **Asaba**. Walking around the campus alone, I met a girl named Precious, who was indeed a precious soul. She welcomed me with joy and quickly introduced me to other people around. *"What is your name, she asked," "I am Micky,"* I answered. *"Micky? That's a pretty nice name"*, she said.

During our discussion and getting to know each other better, I asked how to pay my acceptance fee, and she said she'd show me. We started walking towards the school gate to get a motorbike. On our way, we saw another fresher named Becky. She was also heading to the bank to pay her fees, and I offered to join her on one bike while Precious took another. She seemed rude initially, as I realized most people were not her fans, but she would later become my close friend.

Becky remained quiet throughout the entire ride to the bank. We arrived, paid our fees, and completed the transaction. Later that night, Precious offered me a space to sleep on her bunk since I didn't have a personal bed yet. Before I could even thank her, Becky also provided me with a spot. I decided to stay with Becky, which was how our friendship started.

When Charity finally arrived at school, I noticed she was upset that I had left her behind in **Benin.** We had different struggles, and I couldn't delay my departure for another week, especially since I had nowhere to stay and had already told Val I was going to **Asaba.** I apologized to Charity, explaining that I didn't intend to leave her behind but had no choice. She understood me, and despite the initial misunderstanding, we reconciled, became friends again, and began attending classes together.

Classes started soon, and I attended regularly. My father's company was close to **Asaba,** so I was closer to him than my siblings in **Benin.** I couldn't reach my younger siblings often since they had no phones. I ended up talking to my parents more, and they used me to communicate with each other. When they argued and fought, I had to settle them or become their therapist, which was tough because I had to balance it with school.

It was time for my first-semester exams. I wrote beautifully during my first two examinations, but due to the stress of life, I forgot to write my name and identification number on my script. I had submitted and left the examination hall before I realized I had made a terrible mistake. I panicked a lot. *"There was only one way to fix this,"* I thought. I had to approach the lecturers, own up to my mistake, and beg them to let me correct it. One of them was easy to approach, and he was understanding. The other wanted me to search for the exact pen I used in the examination hall before she let me write my name. It was hard because I didn't remember which pens I had previously used. After several back-and-forths with her, I eventually sorted it out.

My father rarely visited me in school because he was busy with his construction company. He was into borehole projects for smaller villages. Whenever he couldn't make it to school to give me money, I would have to visit him to collect funds.

Similarly, my mother visited him occasionally whenever she could spare a little time, but their encounters often ended in arguments. My mother would accuse him of cheating, citing the presence of other women's clothing in his house. He apologized for his actions on some occasions, but on others, he became angry and expressed a desire to live independently.

Everything happening at home became overwhelming at some point, and I needed someone to talk to. I chose Becky, as she's been my support and safe place. I told her about the stress I was facing, and she listened attentively and advised me to ignore it. But how could I? I was at a crossroads. If I didn't answer my father's calls, he might stop paying my fees or sending money for food, which was not the situation I was looking forward to.

An Encounter That Left Me Speechless

During the second semester of our first year, Precious invited me for a walk one evening to see other students in the boys' hostel. Along the way, she suggested we try a drink. After much persuasion, I agreed despite knowing about my intolerance to alcohol and sugar. She handed me a liquor bottle (Alomo Bitters), and I sipped directly from it. On our way back, I suddenly lost consciousness and fainted. Precious was confused as she could not understand what just happened. In fear, she panicked and ran to seek help from the other girls in the hostel.

I AM MICKY

Amidst the chaos, Faith, known for her protective nature, quickly rushed me to the school clinic. The news spread like wildfire, immediately drawing all my friends and coursemates to the clinic. Even Ese, a coursemate whom I wasn't particularly close to but who liked me as a person because I was young and vibrant, showed genuine concern. She was crying and praying fervently for my recovery while asking God to restore my health and not allow me to die. I could hear her prayers in my subconscious, and somehow, I regained consciousness and woke up. There was jubilation from everyone as I started taking notice of all my friends who were present. Peering into their worried faces, I realized that Becky was absent for unknown reasons. I could not tell what it was, but I believed she did not care.

After leaving the school clinic, my friends rushed me to a laboratory where the technician wasted no time in conducting several tests to determine the primary cause of my sudden fainting. After Precious narrated my ordeal to the medical team at the school clinic, they believed that alcohol couldn't be the sole culprit. They suspected there might be another underlying issue. Recognizing the severity of the situation, Faith took it upon herself to contact my father, who promptly left his company to be by my side. After several scans, the results all showed nothing was wrong with me.

Still not convinced, we sought a second opinion from another laboratory. The new technician suggested that something resembling a stone obstructed my stomach, but it was out. Strangely, when I urinated, he couldn't locate the supposed obstruction. I did not know whether he was right or just said that to make me feel good, but I noticed I felt better while still having minor pains. Despite this, I returned to school, grateful for my friends' care and concern during the ordeal.

When I returned to the hostel, all my friends welcomed me warmly, showering me with care and concern. Precious, in particular, treated me like a baby, feeding me pap and keeping my spirits up with her playful jokes. However, there was tension surrounding Becky as everyone was pissed at her. They believed we were close friends, yet she seemed absent during my ordeal. After much back and forth, Becky apologized, explaining she was busy.

On the other hand, Faith asked me to avoid Becky because she was not a good friend. Despite Faith's warning, I overlooked Becky's absence, as she had always been there to listen to my troubles. Forgiving her seemed like the natural choice for me.

Two days later, I went to the toilet and while defecating, I was startled to see a giant, strange, long worm emerge from my body. I couldn't understand how it had gotten there. I screamed in shock, and then, it dawned on me that this might have been the culprit causing the blockage and discomfort in my body. Seeing it out of my body was all I needed to feel better.

I AM MICKY

The Idea and Shock That Birthed Independence

One night, while reminiscing, an idea struck. I needed to start a side hustle. It was almost the end of my second semester in my first year at the university. The idea was to buy old used Blackberry phones, change the casings to new cheap ones, and sell the phones as refurbished.

I needed to gather solid connections to make this work. So, I contacted my friends and coursemates and told them about my plan, which they welcomed as a good idea. I gathered money, got the phones, fixed them, and started selling them at a reasonable price. Eventually, my efforts paid off, and I made good money. Soon, I became known and famous around the university.

In my second year, I decided to move off-campus for more privacy. When I told Becky about it, she loved the idea. That was how we rented a place together and moved in as roommates. After paying the rent, we didn't have much money to buy a bed. So, we slept on the floor for a few months until we could afford one. I had already started disturbing my father about my second-year school fees.

At that point, I was grateful to have a side hustle because it helped me pay bills and buy food whenever needed until my father reimbursed me. Seeing that I was coping somehow without him, my father called me *"Young Money." "Later, we'll discuss why having a side job is vital in the other chapter."*

My coursemates, Charity and Cordelia, became my lodge mates after they found out that there was a vacant room in the lodge, though they stayed downstairs. This closeness encouraged a tighter bond, and I had the opportunity to learn baking and sewing skills from them. Ese, although not residing in our lodge, lived off-campus, too. Despite the distance, we met regularly and helped each other. We faced challenges and stresses, but I often try to hide mine, preferring to focus on helping

them as we collectively strive for academic success.

After the delays, my dad finally sent the money for my second-year fees, and I paid. Life continued. How I thought everything would be better. Oh, I was wrong! In the coming months, I received the most shocking text message of my life from my father. The text read: *"I have been through a lot because of this family. My business is failing, and I can't do this anymore. I need to focus on myself. I have sent this message to all family members. You people will never hear from me again until the next 10 years."*

I AM MICKY

My fragile heart could not process the information immediately. I was shocked. *"Why did my father return from **Italy** to do this to us again?"* I quickly tried to call his number, but it was genuinely disconnected. That was the last I heard from my father. For the next eight (8) years, he was gone.

I was alone and had to figure out how to finish university. I became depressed, but I didn't understand or know the meaning of the word *depression* till I was 21 years old. I only knew I was sad and that my whole world would be a mess. This incident happened when I was just 17 and was going on to be 18 years old. I went upstairs to my roommate and cried like a child.

Moving on, I continued my side hustle, hoping to make good profits, but sadly, sales were slow. People were getting tired of Blackberry phones and were now switching to Android because of WhatsApp. Immediately, I decided to switch trends and focus on selling Android phones.

I AM MICKY

A Life-Changing Encounter with Micah

While business was moving smoothly, one of the phones I bought had a problem with its battery. I needed to fix it or get a new one, and the best place I knew for that was in **Benin.** This way, I could fix the battery issue and see my siblings. Immediately after arriving in **Benin,** I headed straight to the **New Benin** market. That was where I met a man named Micah. *"He was the man I needed to cross many red seas."* He had just visited **Benin** and was trying to find a bus back to **Lagos,** but he did not know where to find one.

Since I was going in the same direction, I offered to help. We boarded a bus together and made our way to the **UNIBEN** gate. From there, I showed him which bus to take to **Lagos.** He was grateful, took down my number, and we parted ways.

I briefly left for the house to see my siblings after fixing the battery before returning to **Asaba.** The excitement in their eyes was one I would not forget in a hurry. I was excited to have met them in good health. As we sat together, sharing stories and laughter, I realized how much I had missed their presence.

My primary goal in my second year at university was to graduate with a first-class degree. However, I encountered difficulties with chemistry during my first year's first and second semesters, which significantly affected my performance. The lecturer was more interested in extorting money from students over passing us. Many of us were unwilling to comply with this demand, resulting in nearly everyone receiving an **F** grade. This situation posed a significant challenge for me, leading to a growing dislike for the lecturer. Despite excelling in other courses with **A's** and **B's,** I failed his course. Eventually, the lecturer rectified the situation, and I attained a **D** grade. *"Nigerian lecturers can be funny."*

I AM MICKY

My Reality and an Unmerited Favour

My father was truly gone. Slowly, I was coming to terms with my reality. I called my mother to inform her that I would need my school fees for my third year as soon as I rounded up the second year. She promised she would figure it out, although I did not know how she would do it. Time passed, and I was already in my third year at the university. Yet my mother still hadn't come up with the money, and I was worried.

The first few months of the third year's first semester were for my **teaching practice** at a secondary school, which I had already started. I went there every day, teaching and encouraging the students that they could be anything they wanted. But deep down, I felt stressed and hopeless, knowing that I might have to drop out of the university soon.

One evening, I was sitting on my room floor when I got a WhatsApp message from an unknown number. I was curious about who it could be. So, I asked, *"Who is this?"* The reply came, *"It's me, Micah. We met in* **Benin.** *"* Oh, right! Micah! I remembered him now. He said he wanted to thank me for the help I rendered him the other day. I told him he was welcome, and, in return, he asked how I was doing. *"I usually do not complain or ask for favours from anyone, but I felt lost and confused that day."* So, I told him I wasn't doing well. I explained that I was on the verge of dropping out of school because I couldn't afford the fees. *"Oh, that's sad,"* he said. Then he asked, *"How much is the fee?"* I told him it was 44,000 naira (127 euro).

I was shocked when he asked for my bank details and told me to pray for him so he could find the money somehow and send it to me the following week. I had my doubts. I mean, I barely knew this guy. We had only met once. He didn't know me either. Why would he give up so much money to a stranger? But, as the saying goes, *"Seeing is believing."* A week later, he sent the money I needed and exceeded my expectations by sending even more. I was so happy.

I shared the good news with my roommate and my mother and I asked my mother to thank him. She called him to express her gratitude and offered to repay him, but he refused. He insisted it was a gift, and he was willing to help me until I finished university. *"Typical of mothers!"* My mother was curious and wanted to know why he was helping, and he said, *"I do like your daughter. Maybe, after* she's done with university, *I could marry her."* But of course, she has to pray about it and seek God's guidance.

The truth is, from ages 18 to 22, I didn't take my faith seriously. I knew about God but didn't have a personal relationship with Him. However, I was genuinely thankful for the unexpected help that came my way.

Micah funded my education from my third to fourth year. His support secured my academic journey and ignited a sense of responsibility towards my family. I took up the responsibility of my father as I catered for my siblings and mother. His help came just when I needed it the most. Thanks to him, I graduated with a **second-class upper degree,** achieving a remarkable **A+** on the **German grading system**, just a few points shy of a distinction, all at the age of 20.

CHAPTER FOUR

FIRST MILLION

THEY SAY THE first million is always the hardest to earn, but after breaking that barrier, it becomes more straightforward. My journey into **online investment** began around 2016 or 2017. All thanks to Jas, a nurse I was connected to by an online friend when I was sick; online platforms were my go-to for making great friends. Jas contacted me via phone one day, excitedly sharing about an **MMM investment platform.** The investment opportunity promised a 30% monthly return. I became interested immediately because I earned little at work, which was insufficient to care for myself and my family—I earned about 20,000 naira (61 euros) monthly from the food company I was working at. Sometimes, the management staff delays salary payments.

Eager to explore this venture and invest, I decided to find fellow investors. I joined an online community of investors, where I crossed paths with

Freda, the brain behind **Cash Harvesters.** People from different walks of life and professional backgrounds, such as bankers, real estate agents, and lawyers, filled this platform. Freda, for example, was a lawyer.

I began investing and earning a 30% monthly return. Through referrals, I earned a lot of money. I was good at marketing, so getting people to register under me was easy. My roommate and her family also joined, bringing in more investors. While on this, I started learning about **cryptocurrency** for the first time and researching it, although I didn't invest immediately.

However, the **investment** eventually crashed, causing many losses. People lost their income, life savings, and business funds. Fortunately, I had withdrawn 80% of my funds beforehand, sparing me from the worst—*smart investing means knowing when to exit the investment market.* It was a tough time for everyone, but we found solace in the

Cash Harvesters' group, comforting each other through the trying time.

A New Proposal

A group of guys proposed a new business investment opportunity to Freda, the group's leader, who then shared it with everyone. Many, primarily women, agreed to invest, myself included. However, this investment later turned out to be an intentional scam. Consequently, we all suffered losses, leaving Freda so disappointed and embarrassed. She had always strived for profit, not loss, for the group members. An idea struck me as I watched everyone in the group complain, particularly women. I thought, *"Perhaps I could assist them in recovering their losses."* Doubts surfaced. *"Could I do it?"* Despite my uncertainties, I gathered courage, approached the group, and asked those who had lost money to indicate. After they showed up, I told them I would provide a link to join a new group to collectively strategize on recovering their money.

They all joined the group, including Freda. That was the first time I had direct contact with her. *"What is your plan to recover the money?"* she asked. *"I don't have any plans at the moment,"* I responded, *"but we will get our money back."* After retiring for the night, an idea struck me. I decided to reach out to Micah. Remember Micah? Yes, you should. Micah worked with the **Economic and Financial Crimes Commission (EFCC).** *"I can tell you for free that most Nigerians fear those who work in the law enforcement agency."* I called him and explained the situation. *"Please, I want you to help these women recover their money. Do something like threatening the thieves with legal action,"* I said. After listening to all I had to say, in his defense, he said, *"Micky, I give you the authority to use my name and rank to threaten them. If they do not listen and refund the money, I will take over the situation and find them."*

So, I became a detective and began googling their names to see if I could find any useful information about them that would make the work easier for Micah. There were three guys in question. I discovered the name of their university and found additional photos of them on various social platforms. With enough information, I wrote them a direct message saying, *"Hi, I am Micky. Ten other women and I lost our money to you, and we want all the money back."* Upon reading my message, they laughed and responded, *"How brave!!"*

I sent them all the information I had gathered and warned them that my friend, who works with a law enforcement agency, would track them down, take legal action, and ensure they paid. It was funny how they didn't take me seriously at first. Then, I brought Micah on board. He called them to clarify that we were serious and wouldn't back down until everyone received their money. After the constant dialogues, being left with no choice, and seeing how serious we were, they decided they would refund us.

To my delight, Micah told me they had agreed to send me the money. Overjoyed, I rushed to inform the women in the group, assuring them we'd receive our refund that day. True to their word, the entire sum was sent to me, which I promptly distributed among the women. They could not believe it as their hearts were filled with joy. They prayed for me while expressing their gratitude. That was a proud moment, as this experience brought me closer to Freda. Inspired by it, I eventually decided to launch my **investment platform,** which was a **Digital Ajo.**

The Launch of My Investment Platform & New Hope for My Family

Dinero, Dinero, that's what they call money in **Spanish.** The situation in Nigeria was terrible, and everyone wanted some *Dinero*. So, I decided to take the dive and launch an **investment platform.** I contacted Jas and proposed the idea to him. *"Would you like to join me?"* I asked. He eagerly agreed. I explained to him that we needed ₦250,000 to kick-start the venture—finding five people willing to invest ₦50,000 each. Without delay, he promised to find those five individuals who later became investors.

True to his word, he delivered, and I communicated with them via voice notes (VN). They never saw my face, but my voice was enough to earn their trust. In return for their **investment,** we promised them a 150% profit and priority treatment for being early believers in the project. With the funds secured, I began contacting developers who happened to be **Indians.** However, they only accepted cryptocurrency as payment. Luckily, in 2017, Bitcoin was relatively cheap, and I had about 0.5 BTC. I used 0.3 BTC to pay the developers while the five investors and I marketed ahead of the business launch. The project was very hyped, especially within the **Cash Harvesters group.**

The **Indians** were ready to deliver the website to us for testing and launch. I named the Digital Ajo **FP**; it's a shortened name anyway. Finally, it was launched and proved to be successful.

I managed and operated it from my tiny room in Asaba.

I made my first million from this platform, which ran for a while, with members enjoying their benefits. However, the model was not sustainable enough. I wish I had known better because if one person defaulted on payment, it led to backlogs. It was not easy to run as I was running the back-end of the website administrator with Jas as co-administrator while also acting as customer care. I couldn't sleep some nights as I would eventually fall sick due to stress.

However, I kept to my word and delivered 150% profit to investors while other members of the **investment group** I belonged to earned significant profits, too. Additionally, my roommate and her family invested in this and benefited; they were happy to recover all the huge sum they had lost to MMM through the **investment**.

I took on huge responsibilities at home, and from my accumulated profits, I decided to call my family to help them further. It had been a long time since I had seen them, though I tried to always communicate with them. I knew they were having a hard time, so my first thought was to open a business for my mother. I called her and said, *"I have just done a business that proved effective. I would like to open you a business. Give me a list of items you will need for it, and I will fund it completely"*. She hesitated initially, concerned about the source of my sudden wealth. I reassured her that my earnings were legitimate and I was not involved in anything illegal.

After much persuasion, I opened a food sale business for her. Meanwhile, my younger siblings were nearing the completion of their senior secondary school education, gearing up for their final exams. I ensured they had everything necessary to register for it. I encouraged them to gain entrepreneurial skills, drawing from my experiences at 14. Thankfully, they heeded my advice—my sister chose to go to the same skills school I attended while my brother pursued sewing. Eventually, they both learned how to sew in the future due to my sister's love for fashion. I contacted my elder brothers and offered to help by sending them money for financial support. It again brought joy to our family once more, and happiness returned. I gave them hope.

Greed, Friendship, and Its Lesson

One morning, my roommate, Becky, approached me, expressing her desire for a larger share of my business profits. She argued that since she was present when I started the business in our room, she deserved a more significant cut. Specifically, she demanded 50% more than what she currently received. I firmly explained that I wouldn't entertain such a request as it would never happen. This business was my idea, and I had already done well in sharing my profits with her and her family.

To my surprise, she resorted to threats, claiming she would involve the police and accuse me of running an unregistered business. Her anger was noticeable. Wow! This experience taught me never to forget the saying, *"You never truly know someone until you do business with them."*

At that moment, my roommate received a call from a woman named Uche, who had invested in the **Digital Ajo platform, FP.** My roommate spoke with Uche, who expressed frustration in not getting her money from the investment. She said the system matched her to pay my roommate, which she generously did, but the payer refused to pay her when it was her turn to get paid. She was frustrated and no longer interested and wanted her money back.

Surprisingly, Becky, whom I had expected to handle the situation calmly, did the opposite due to her anger towards me. She told Uche, *"The owner is here, and I can give you her number. You should do what you like with her."* I responded in the background, *"You can give her my number."* Almost immediately, she called, clearly furious. I tried to calm her, but it seemed not to be working. She revealed she was a member of the **Cash Harvesters**

group and feared that she may have lost her investment. Acknowledging her frustration, I told her the investment comes with a risk, as clearly stated in the disclaimer. My words seemed to strike a nerve as she angrily threatened, *"I am going to kidnap you and your friend, lock you both up somewhere dark, and you will never see anyone again."* I laughed. It's a habit of mine to always find humor, even in serious discussions. I jokingly told Uche, *"I hope I can at least get breakfast while locked up."* She laughed, teasing me, *"You're weird."* I was happy I could make light of the situation while promising her that I would give her back her complete money as she did not have to kidnap anybody.

We decided to continue our conversation on WhatsApp while I figured out how to solve her issue. We engaged in a captivating conversation. During the discussion, Uche asked why my friend gave up on me that way, but you, in turn, defended her during the phone call. I emphasized the significance of my friendships, stating that maintaining solid bonds with people is essential to me.

I'll discuss Uche's role again in another chapter, but it's worth noting that this was how we met.

It was my birthday five months later, and Uche ordered a cake for me. She instructed me to pick it up at one of Asaba's top cake shops. On getting there, I was captivated by the atmosphere and wanted to intern with them. I quickly seized the opportunity and expressed my interest in interning with them to the management. To my delight, they agreed, and I commenced an internship program and ended up working with them for two years. This job was my **first official appointment** after my bachelor's degree.

Blessings in Friendship

MMM, the first **investment platform** that crashed, made a comeback, and I aimed to approach it more strategically this time. I devised using multiple accounts and withdrawing funds as fast as possible before it had another issue. Seeking cooperation, I contacted friends and family, proposing to use their accounts to receive the funds. Through Becky, my roommate, I got across to her sister, Ify, who connected me with Naomi, her friend. Graciously, Naomi offered her account, having heard a lot about me in the past and expressing great excitement about getting to know me.

The connection with Naomi turned out great, and she is now like a sister to me, despite not sharing the same mother. Hailing from **Benin** and residing with her aunt, Naomi exuded kindness and respect. Our bond deepened even after our business deal was over. Uche and Naomi became life-purpose friends to me; I needed to know them to continue their roles in my life. I owe my gratitude to Ify and Becky. God used them to place Uche and Naomi in my life, intentionally and unintentionally.

A Second Investment Platform - Meeting Otis and Paul

Otis was my first business partner, and our connection was solely online, with no physical encounter. Despite this, he was lovely as he exuded warmth and charm. I am trying to remember how we had our first contact. But I remember he wanted to collaborate with me to launch an **investment platform** called **Keyfunders**—a sustainable one. Together, we embarked on this journey, working on it, naming it, and engaging a **Nigerian** developer. We didn't want to pay so much, so we found a **Nigerian** who could do it for us at a cheaper rate, a decision that would later backfire.

Vine was the name of our developer, and our shared vision was to make this investment last for a long time. Otis drove a desire to help people with this platform by enabling them to benefit from each other. Our plan involved rotating the investment and sharing profits with each participating member every four days.

Also, Otis possessed exceptional skills as a spokesperson and salesman, talents that continue to serve him well as a successful businessman today. His gift of public speaking has allowed him to excel in marketing. At the same time, I focused on back-end jobs as a technical expert, leveraging my computer programming knowledge and ensuring the programs' smooth running. I worked closely with the programmer Vine while Otis started marketing and elevated our Telegram group from 20 people to over a thousand. He truly excelled in his role.

In the marketing process, we met Paul, a sweet yet somewhat troublesome individual. With his background in writing and knowledge of the law, he brought a unique perspective to our team. Together, we formed a formidable group, with Micky as the *tech expert*, Vine as the *programmer,* Otis as the *great marketer,* and Paul as the *poet and talented writer*. With such diverse skills, we couldn't have failed.

However, shortly after the platform's launch, we encountered unexpected problems. A bug in the programming code created a linkage, allowing someone, somewhere, to siphon funds without our knowledge. Remember, our intention for this platform was to be sustainable, but unfortunately, that wasn't the case. A programming glitch caused every "Provide Help" (PH) to be matched with a 2X "Get Help" (GH) transaction to a bug account. This error went unnoticed by our team for weeks. Then, one day, a woman in our Telegram group raised suspicions, suggesting that we were scammers and that a particular account received funds daily. Otis, quick to act, addressed the situation promptly to prevent chaos. Aware of the damaging implications of the word scam, he carefully handled the situation. Recognizing the urgency, Otis called me immediately. His trust in me was evident as he spoke, *"Micky, there's an issue we must address. We can't afford to lose our investors' trust. We have to investigate the account receiving these consistent payments."*

The Challenge

That was the moment of truth! Not once did I doubt Otis's trust in me, especially considering my role in managing the website's back-end operations.

I knew he had complete confidence in me. *"This is a serious issue,"* I replied, trying to maintain composure. *"I'll contact the programmer and carry out a thorough investigation."* After contacting Vine, he reassured me that such a situation was unlikely. Yet, my instincts as a detective kicked in. Deciding to take matters into my own hands, I conducted a comprehensive audit of the account that had been provided and got help.

To my astonishment, I discovered an account that had made no contributions but had received more than anyone else. Temi was the owner of the account. This woman stressed the hell out of me. Remember, I had helped people recover stolen funds in the past. I was sure I could do it again. Oh, man! I couldn't have been more mistaken. I became increasingly frustrated as it became clear that Temi was not what I expected—a somewhat disagreeable young lady. I began to carry out my research on her. I had her name, address, and account number. I got this from her registered information on our website.

With all the information I needed, I called Temi to talk with her. *"Hi Temi, this is one of the founders of Keyfunders. I want to speak to you shortly if that is okay."* Temi ended the call. I tried again, but this time I started to get pissed. She picked, and I screamed at her. *"Do you want to damage my reputation? I would not let you do that. I will find you, and you will pay."* She responded, *"Find me if you can."* A challenge? I never give up, and I love a good challenge.

At this time in my personal life, I was handling my university final clearance and registration for the **National Youth Service Corps (NYSC).** I combined the stress of tracking Temi, completing clearance procedures, and managing the website's back end at home. Concurrently, I transitioned from my previous job to a role at an **investment company** specializing in stocks and options trading. While with them, I acquired valuable insights before resigning and focusing on running my **investment platform** from home.

I AM MICKY

The positive outcome of my detective work was that I gathered sufficient information about Temi. I tried everything possible to reach her on the phone. But when it proved abortive, I resorted to messaging her on WhatsApp. *"Hey, I have your school's name, picture, and family member's name. If you don't refund what you took from the company, I'll speak to them,"* I said, frustration evident in my tone. She responded casually, *"I didn't steal; a glitch in your website worked in my favor. I earned it fair and square, so I'm keeping it."* She remained adamant despite my attempts to tell her *"favors"* did not work that way.

Meanwhile, the suspected *scam situation* Otis was handling in the group escalated. Rumors circulated that we had deliberately engineered a bug to defraud investors. Unable to manage the growing panic, we had to seek Paul's help. Paul had a lovely voice and spoke calmly like a lady. His soothing voice and eloquent writing style worked wonders immediately. He took control of the group, transforming its chaotic atmosphere into tranquility.

After enduring enough threats and conflicts, Temi conceded and agreed to refund 70% of the money. Exhausted from the ordeal, I accepted this compromise and agreed to her terms. Subsequently, we returned the refunded money to the **investment platform,** ending the turbulent situation.

National Youth Service Corps Called

Soon enough, my call-up letter for NYSC was out. I had just been posted with my roommate to **Northern Nigeria** to serve my country. It wasn't the best option, but I had no choice. I told Otis and Paul I would leave the entire platform to their care as I could not use my phone or computer during camp. They agreed to this plan and took over the management of the whole **investment platform** while I was away. While preparing for this next stage of my life, I thought visiting my family in **Benin** before I left was better. The following week, I traveled to **Benin**. I remember conversing with my mother about wanting to invest in landed properties. Luckily, when I arrived, I noticed she had found a good one. Instead of buying just one, I opted to buy two lands—this transaction I did at age 20 and left for **Abuja** the following week.

CHAPTER FIVE

LIFE DURING NYSC

I WAS ON the move again, excited and ready for something new. It felt like fate had interfered, as my roommate and I found ourselves in nearly the same place. Despite Becky and I applying for NYSC on different days, we ended up in the same state for service, **Nasarawa State.** I had never visited the **North** before, as this was my first time. The journey promised excitement as I anticipated discovering the entirely different world of the **Northern region** of **Nigeria.** My roommate and I embarked on a 6-hour bus journey from **Asaba,** chatting and looking through the window as the view changed. I had no family members or friends in the **North.** Luckily for me, my roommate had her family residing in **Abuja.**

We arrived at the park around 9 PM, where her brother picked us up and took us to their place.

Our spirits soared with anticipation for the days ahead. The next day, the adventure continued as we headed to camp in **Nasarawa State.** Boarding yet another bus, we embarked on the two-hour journey to the campground in **Keffi, Nasarawa State.** Still unsure of the future, we were ready for whatever came our way.

Life in Camp

Camp life? Wow! There, I experienced the most fun of my life. It felt like escaping from the stressful world into a joy-filled place. There were people of all shapes and sizes, creating a vibrant atmosphere. Amidst everyone, I noticed a girl I admired during registration but hesitated to approach her. I later learned her name was Brown. Although I was too shy to initiate a conversation, Becky introduced us. *"Hi, I'm Becky, and this is Micky,"* she said. Brown responded warmly, introducing herself to us in return. That was how I had my first conversation with Brown. I also met a guy named Michael, whom we are still friends to date. I started talking to him because he always sang me this funny song, "*Micky (2X), you are so fine, you so fine. You blow my mind, hey Micky.*" He liked me and was very friendly to me.

My roommate and I were surprised that we shared the same platoon alongside Brown and Michael. Five days later, during the morning parade,

the Group Coordinator suggested we form a **Drama Group,** of which Micheal was the leader. We eagerly complied, which was how the four of us, along with others, formed the group. Micheal, Brown, and I began spending more time together as the camp progressed. During breaks, Brown graciously shared her stories and experiences with me, and through our interactions, she encouraged me to become more outspoken.

End of Camp Life

It was now three weeks, and the time had come to bid farewell to camp life and return to the reality of the service year. During camp, I pleaded with Micah to help me process my relocation to **Lagos** because I wanted to separate from my roommate. *"Having known her for six years, our friendship was collapsing."* I needed a new start in a new state where I had a few people around me, but this plan failed. Nevertheless, despite the failure of my relocation, I still felt grateful for having made friends with Brown, as we promised to keep in touch.

As camp life ended, it was time for me to head back to **Abuja.** I had just turned down my first **Place of Primary Assignment (PPA)** because it didn't appeal to me. At this point, I knew I had to redeploy. Feeling clueless and lost, I did not know where to go or what to do next, as I had no connection in **Abuja** or support. Then, an opportunity arose when Becky's sister, who worked at the **Nnamdi Azikiwe International Airport, Abuja,** suggested that Becky seek a posting there. I followed suit and asked to be posted alongside her, as my options were limited. To redeploy, I got my Redeployment Letter and Remita ready and submitted it for stamping at the **NYSC Secretarial Office** at **Keffi** while waiting for authorization. I eagerly embraced this chance, and soon enough, we received our posting letters to serve at the airport and were ecstatic about the opportunity.

Facing a New Reality

We dressed up the following day and headed to the airport together. Becky's sister awaited us at the door. Upon seeing us, she said, *"The airport manager informed me that there is only one spot available for one person, but let's give it a try. Both of you come with me."* We followed her up the stairs. It was my second time at an airport. The first time, I accompanied a friend of Micah's to the **international airport in Lagos State.** He was traveling to the **Netherlands.** Due to Micah's law enforcement status, we had the privilege of accompanying him to the final checkpoint. As he prepared to board the plane, I hugged him tightly and shed tears. Those tears were not because I was going to miss him. I didn't know him much, but I knew I wanted to travel for my Master's degree to a different country someday. So, on this second visit to the airport, I felt that same longing, but this time, my focus was on serving my country.

Becky's sister instructed us to wait as we approached the airport manager's office. She went inside the office and spoke to him on our behalf before asking us to come in. We entered, and he said, *"Oh, the two of you came. Well, I only have space for one person."* I quickly suggested, *"Sir, it would be nice if you could accommodate both of us. I don't mind which department I'm assigned to, as I don't have many options."* He replied, *"I must choose someone fairly if I am to do so. I'll write 'yes' and 'no' on two pieces of paper. Whoever picks 'yes' will be my new corps member, and the one who picks 'no' will need to find another place to serve."* That sounded fair to us, so we agreed.

I AM MICKY

He wrote *'yes'* and *'no'* on the papers, folded them, and asked us to choose. I wanted to give my friend a better chance, so I asked her to pick first. She chose the first paper, leaving me with the second one. I had the *'yes'* when we unfolded them, while she had the *'no.'* I wasn't happy about it, thinking, *"My friend will be upset with me."* I quickly chipped in, *"Sir, it is only fair that you pick my friend. Her sister works here. I can find somewhere else."* He replied, *"You're such a generous soul. I will accept both of you to work with me."* I couldn't believe it. My excitement was over the moon. That's how I ended up serving at the **International Airport, Abuja, at the VIP Lounge.**

Becky and I found accommodation 20km from the airport and moved in together. While working at the airport, I met amazing people. One of them was Rita, who worked alongside me at the **VIP Lounge.** We instantly connected and formed a strong friendship, always looking out for each other. Additionally, I met and befriended Dammy, a wonderful person who is incredibly down-to-earth.

Although the job was not easy, it was fun. I interacted with colleagues who held permanent positions and had the opportunity to encounter many prominent government officials. I admired the conduct of passengers at the airport—most were very well-dressed and pleasant-smelling.

Turn of Event — Plans for Master's Degree

One day during my night shift, while scrolling through Facebook, I came across a post from a very old friend, Precious, whom I had met online on 2go (a chatting site in 2007). We had lost contact, but somehow, we reconnected on Facebook. I noticed she had recently moved to **Germany.** Fascinated, I went to her inbox and messaged her, *"Hey, I can see you're in **Germany** now. What are you doing there?"* She replied, *"Oh, I'm here for my Master's."* This disclosure caught my curiosity, and I delved deeper into the conversation, gathering information about **Germany** from her. **Germany** had never been part of my plans; I had always pictured pursuing my Master's in English-speaking countries like **Canada** or the **United Kingdom.** However, her insights sparked my interest.

Upon returning home the following day, I discussed the idea with Micah. He had always encouraged me to further my education, and I was delighted by the opportunity. He suggested I find someone who could assist with the admission process. I contacted a few people whom I knew from my online **investment group.** One of them mentioned her uncle's involvement in facilitating admissions for international students to Germany and **Canada.** I contacted her and obtained her uncle's contact information, which I forwarded to Micah. Micah and I never spoke about the subject again as I continued enjoying my service year while making new friends and connections.

A New Girl at Work

During one of my afternoon shifts, a girl arrived accompanied by the Airport's Operations Manager. She exuded a bright and confident aura. I quickly told my colleague, Rita, that we had to make friends with this girl who looked like a new employee. We later found out that she was there for an internship. Her name was Jay, and she always smiled. She worked at the front desk of the airport. Anytime I walked home, I waved at her, and she waved back, but we never spoke. A week later, I noticed her absence from the front desk and wondered whether her internship had concluded so soon. She wasn't available for two weeks, and then, one evening after my shift, I saw her again as I headed home.

Upon greeting her, we engaged in our first conversation. *"Hey, where have you been?"* I inquired. With a hug, she asked, *"Did you notice I wasn't here for two weeks?"* *"Oh, yes! I did,"* I responded. We exchanged numbers and initiated chats. Laughter filled our conversations, and gradually, Jay confided in me about her housing issue. At that time, I stayed alone following my recent separation from Becky, who had moved in with her sister. Feeling lonely, I offered Jay to stay at my place. She offered to visit first before moving into my apartment. After two visits, she finally moved in. This arrangement allowed her to remain in **Abuja** until the completion of her internship. Coincidentally, I had a very calm neighbor, Ray, who always kept to himself and rarely spoke to anyone. We only said *hi's and hellos.* Upon Jay's arrival, interactions with my neighbor strengthened. Ray, **a first-class graduate** from a university in the **United Kingdom,** had returned to **Nigeria** to be closer to his family. He had a perfect job and was a pretty nice guy. When we got talking, we enjoyed our time with him. He consistently gave positive vibes and offered valuable advice. Sometimes, we went to **Shoprite** (a big shopping mall in Abuja) to get groceries.

About six months into my stay in **Abuja,** Micah reached out to me unexpectedly. *"Remember the contact you gave me for the guy who can assist you in securing admission in **Germany**?"* he asked. Surprised, I responded, *"Yes, I remember."* Micah continued, *"Well, I contacted the person today, and we discussed about it. He provided me with the* *details of the required fee for processing the admission, which I have already paid in full to initiate the process. You can now send all your documents to him, and he will proceed further.* " I felt a rush of excitement mixed with shock. I had assumed Micah had forgotten about this promise, and consequently, I wasn't as motivated anymore. I told Ray about this information and that I was ready to do my Master's abroad like him. He was so excited for me.

The Hustle

NYSC was drawing to a close. We were preparing for the final **Community Development Service (CDS)** and clearance to receive our NYSC certificate. While at the CDS location, I received an email from the **University of Kassel**, a school to which the agent has applied, stating that I had been offered admission and was to resume in October. The email came in July, and I couldn't help but smile. The first people I reached out to were Jay and Ray, who felt like family to me. I also called Micah to share the news and express gratitude for kick-starting the process.

After completing my CDS duties, I took a taxi home excitedly. It was finally happening! I would soon be pursuing my Master's degree. The joy was inexplicable. I decided to visit home again to spend time with my family, collect some original documents, and rectify the misspelling of my name on my Bachelor's certificate. This error needed correction at my university. At age 22, this was my first airplane use, and I was super excited.

Boarding the **Airmax** flight to **Benin**, I found the experience beautiful. I captured many pictures, savored the moments, and created many memories. I didn't stay in **Benin** for too long as I had to return to **Abuja**. Upon arrival, I promptly contacted the agent overseeing my admission process, and we discussed the next step. He mentioned I needed to block an account in **Germany,** a detail I was somewhat prepared for, thanks to a conversation with Precious on Facebook.

A Block Account is the amount of money an immigrant needs to support themselves for one year in Germany. The system programs the release of 750 euros every month until the completion of 12 months.

However, the exact amount required shocked me. I needed approximately 8640 euros (equivalent to 3.5 million naira in 2018, with an exchange rate of 1 euro = 400 naira). It was quite a lot of money. Light-heartedly, I joked about it with my friends, mentioning that if I couldn't gather the funds for the trip, I might use the 1 million I already had to purchase a car and work as a taxi driver in **Abuja.** After all, I wasn't ready to return home without securing a job.

I had access to 2.5 million naira in the past, but I've used about 800,000 naira to support myself and my family. I had approximately 1.2 million naira in savings left. However, I found myself in need of 3.5 million naira. How was I to come up with that money in that short time—four months, to be precise?

I needed to raise 2.5 million naira, including my flight fare. Phew! To be honest, I found myself quite overwhelmed. I began to process the admission acceptance and find an appointment for my visa interview. *"It is a requirement to have your account funded before going for a visa interview."* Still, as I mentioned, I couldn't raise the money quickly, not even before my visa interview, scheduled for August 28, 2018.

Desperate, I began scrambling for funds, reaching out to everyone I knew: family, friends, acquaintances, colleagues, even strangers online. Despite my extensive efforts, money was not forthcoming. Nonetheless, Ray offered encouragement, urging me not to lose hope, and promised to help me with whatever he could find. Jay stood by my side all through, soliciting funds on my behalf. Meanwhile,

I AM MICKY

Dammy was conversing with her boyfriend about securing a loan for me. I remained open to selling my lands while my mother searched for potential buyers. It was undeniably a challenging period for me. Amidst it all, I contacted Micah to update him on the progress and information I had gathered. His response was reassuring; he pledged to support me fully. He went as far as saying, *"I'll give you the 2 million naira. You just need to come up with the additional five hundred thousand naira to complement your 1 million naira."*

Trip to Lagos

I booked a flight to **Lagos** for my interview. I had all the necessary documents except for proof of a blocked account. Upon arrival, Micah picked me up. Together, we had several appointments with loan sharks, but they all changed their minds when we got there. Micah had plans to sell his land, but the potential buyers backed out at the last minute. Eventually, I asked Micah to drop me off on the Island as I wanted to visit Freda—Freda from the

Cash Harvester group. I wanted to meet with her. When we finally met, she was so lovely and welcoming.

After many pleasantries and catching up on old times, I returned to the mainland and checked into a hotel. Micah was waiting for me there. That night, I dedicated myself to preparing for the interview, with Micah's help as he role-played as the *interviewer*. The following day, he prayed with me and dropped me off at the Embassy. As we arrived at the entrance, a lengthy line greeted us, *a familiar sight to anyone who has visited the* **German Embassy in Lagos.** Positioned at the back of the line, I couldn't help but notice the stern presence of the gateman. Everyone feared him so much. I had heard tales about him— how he had the power to turn a good day sour, just like he had done for so many others. Determined to avoid confrontation, I remained cautious and kept to myself, mindful of potential issues. However, my attention shifted to a girl at the front of the third line, near the entrance, who had made a mistake with her documents. The gateman's irritation was noticeable as he reacted rudely to her error. He said, *"You're not serious and don't deserve to travel."* Then, sighting me, he beckoned, *"You there, come to the front and replace this unserious girl."* I was surprised. *"Me?"* I stammered. *"Yes, you, before I change my mind,"* he announced.

The Interview

I walked up to the front and found myself third in line, but as luck would have it, I ended up being the second person to enter the Embassy, jumping ahead from what could have been the 15th spot to the 3rd spot. Once inside, I took a seat and waited for my turn. I was supposed to enter the first room, but someone else did. So, the official redirected me to the middle room instead—a decision that later made sense. Stepping inside, I was suddenly overwhelmed by a panic attack. I was shaking because I knew I had an incomplete document. Yet, I whispered, *"Hey Micky, you're here now. Stay bold! Stay brave! Be Micky."*

I AM MICKY

The interviewer, Jonathan, saw my anxiety and said, *"Take your time and let me know when you are ready to start."* After putting myself together, I affirmed that I was ready—his patience and kindness made me braver. *"Thank you, Johnathan, if you ever get to read this."* Then he began questioning me, and I responded confidently. *"I still have my practice book from 2018."* He commended my composure and expressed his deep impression of how I managed myself. He asked why I didn't have the block account confirmation, and I told him I was working on it and that if they gave me a chance, I could send it to them later when I had it. He didn't seem optimistic about this comment because this was an essential requirement that I didn't fulfill. He then asked if I had any knowledge of German, to which I replied that I had some basic understanding, having started learning through **Duolingo.** After exchanging pleasantries, we bid each other farewell, and I exited, marking the end of the interview.

I AM MICKY

My Fate

Exhausted yet relieved, I returned to the hotel. This time, I confided in Micah, pleading, *"I urgently need this money. It's crucial for my documents, and the Embassy is asking about it."* Micah explained that clearing a backlog of car containers caused his slow business. Feeling motivated, I suggested a trip to see my friend Uche in **Lagos** despite her playful joke about wanting to kidnap me in the past. As a banker, she might be able to assist with a loan. Micah agreed, and that night, he drove me to Uche's house. Despite her warm welcome, she said she couldn't help as I had no asset *(collateral)* to borrow against the loan. I begged her so much, but she said she could do nothing.

Disheartened, I returned to the hotel. Micah then proposed a risky venture, asking me to accompany him to the seaport to clear the cars that his suppliers had shipped in. This trip was dangerous as we rode bikes between heavy-duty containers. Each time I entered **Lagos,** I felt a sense of chaos and discomfort. The bustling city amplifies stress and survival instincts. My visit to the seaport with two EFCC men—Micah and his colleague intensified my negative perception of **Lagos.** While I knew about Micah's car-clearing business, experiencing the stress firsthand was eye-opening. I had accompanied him once to the **Benin Republic,** where we jointly cleared three cars. I sold one of those cars to my friend Jas, the nurse.

Surprisingly, clearing vehicles in **Benin Republic** was far smoother than in **Lagos,** which gave an *Indaboski vibe* (a stressful atmosphere). Interacting with clearing agents and customs officers in **Lagos** was always challenging, as they were consistently rude and corrupt. Our stress just started. We were ready each morning at 5 AM sharp, braving the congested traffic en route to the seaport. **Lagos** is notorious for its traffic jams, and I often felt car sick. Despite the discomfort, I was determined to support Micah and navigate the situation for my benefit. Thus, I persevered through it all.

During this process, I witnessed levels of corruption that I had never encountered before. I was getting exhausted as some arrangements were not going according to plan. One day after returning from the seaport, I told Micah, *"Micah, I have no time left. The Embassy just emailed, confirming they're ready to approve my visa. However, they require confirmation of the block account and my international passport to finalize the visa stamping process."* *He wanted to see the email, and I showed him, the* weight overwhelming me. I pleaded with him again, *"Please, help me out. You initiated this process. Why has it become so stressful now?"* He hesitated, responding, *"I have the money, but I'm not ready to release it yet. You'll have to wait."* Frustration swelled within me. *"Wait? I've already waited a week, and my final NYSC clearance is pending. How much longer can I wait? Time is not on my side."* Despite my insistence, Micah avoided further discussion on the matter. However, I knew he possessed the funds; we never kept such matters hidden from each other.

After several pleadings and persuasion, the two million naira was eventually acquired from Micah, though under unfavorable circumstances. The loan from Micah totaled the available money to three million naira, leaving me with a shortfall of five hundred thousand naira. I went straight to the bank and transferred the money from my private account to the **German** block account in **Germany.** It took about three days for the funds to reflect—the next crucial question persisted: How could I obtain the remaining amount of 500,000 naira?

CHAPTER SIX

A CRY FOR HELP

MAY YOU NEVER face your battles alone. While I had known God through attending church, I had not truly experienced His presence. I was in the most challenging phase of life I have ever encountered. Despite having dreams, visions, and aspirations, I felt alone navigating life's obstacles. This isolation weighed heavily on me, leading to a deep sadness. With each passing day, I have only deepened my unhappiness, particularly as I struggled to meet financial obligations. I was unhappy as I wasn't coming up with the remaining balance. It felt as though my world was crashing around me, and I found myself consumed by tears and regret, questioning why I had been born into such circumstances. *"Why me? Why should I fight this battle for so long? Now, I can change something in my life, and no family member can help me"*. This fear became a constant refrain in my thoughts. *"I felt like I was failing, but God was teaching me some lessons."* All this time, I was holding on to my strength and that of Micah, but all this was failing. I needed to focus on the source, God, for all the resources to align.

In despair, I turned to God through music for solace as my mother did in the past, particularly songs of hope through gospel music. These melodies became a source of comfort, accompanying me throughout my day and into the night. I mostly played *"If All I Can Say is Jesus" by Dunsin Oyekan and "Cheta (Wait)" by Ada Ehi.* Tears flowed freely from my eyes as I listened to these melodies and began pouring my heart to God. *"My mother knows you,"* I cried out. *"She praised you every day. Why, then, must her daughter endure such suffering? I have sacrificed everything for my family, dedicating my time and resources, even when I had little to spare. Why must I continue to plead for a better life?"*

Day after day, I did this and received no response or solace from God. Silence met my inquiries. *"Why me?"* I implored. *"Why put so much burden on me and leave me hanging?"* Yet, there was no answer. *"Is the God I call on dead? Does He exist? Is my mother just following someone who can do nothing for her?"* With the responsibility of providing for a household of three weighing heavily on me, I questioned God's presence and guidance.

An Answered Prayer

Jay had returned to school the previous week, leaving me alone in the house. A few weeks later, when she arrived back, I hugged her tightly and broke down in tears. *"I wish I could help you,"* she said sympathetically. *"I know you need this, but I can't help now, I tried to contact a few NGOs on your behalf, but they can't help you either."* Then, at that moment, I heard a voice urging me, *"Call Uche!"* Though I didn't know who spoke or why, I felt forced to heed the advice. *"I had previously called Uche before to beg her, and even my mother has called on my behalf, but she had always said NO to a loan."* I had every reason not to call her again, but I obeyed the voice. With reluctance, I reached for my phone and dialed Uche's number. When she picked up, I told her, *"Hi Uche, I am sorry to disturb you again. I still need your help. I've managed to gather 3 million naira. All I need now is 500,000 naira to complete it. Can you please help me with this?"* To my surprise, Uche responded, *"Yes! I'll give you the money tomorrow. I'll take a loan against my salary and send it to you. If you don't pay me back, I won't receive a salary for the following year."* Grateful, I promised her that I would repay every cent with interest. True to her word, she sent me the money the next day.

My excitement knew no bounds as I finally had the last piece of the puzzle. This was the relief I needed. With just four days left to submit proof of the money and my passport to the Embassy, I hurriedly went to the bank to transfer the remaining amount required for the German account. However, I found myself 40 euros short due to the exchange rate. In a stroke of luck, I reached out to Precious, my Facebook friend, and asked if she could send 40 euros to the bank account in Germany. She graciously agreed to help, and within a remarkably short time, Precious sent the 40 euros. However, Precious and I were anxious. This anxiety is because transfers to German accounts from a third-world country typically take about three days to reflect, and I had just transferred the last 500,000 naira to the account that morning. We worried it would not arrive in time as the previous 3 million naira took three days to come into the account. But to my amazement, the funds arrived in less than one day—an unexpected blessing that I attributed to divine intervention.

When I shared the news with Precious, she was surprised, remarking, *"You have a special grace. There's something different about you."* With a smile, I told her, *"I've been talking to God, and He didn't want to leave me alone. He knew I needed Him the most now."* Everything previously delayed worked as I waited patiently for the official bank confirmation of the total sum.

I AM MICKY

A Divine Help

With the total amount and confirmation from the German bank secured, a new challenge arose. I had to present my passport and bank confirmation at the Embassy in **Lagos,** which required another trip. However, this clashed with my commitment to attending my **Passing Out Parade (POP)** in **Abuja** and collecting my **NYSC Certificate.** Faced with this dilemma, I found myself torn between fulfilling both obligations. Adding to the complication, I lacked the funds for another flight booking, leaving me to find an alternative solution.

The Holy Spirit, whom I now recognize, was guiding me. He instructed me to proceed to the airport and wait at a designated corner. Following His direction, I arrived at the International Airport in **Abuja** and positioned myself in the local airport area. As I scanned through the boarding passengers, the Holy Spirit drew my attention to a seemingly rugged individual, a choice I wouldn't have made on my own. However, prompted by the Holy Spirit, I approached him. His name was Koko. Inquiring if he was bound for **Lagos State,** he confirmed and mentioned stopping at the second gate of the **Lagos Island.** *"That was where I wanted him to drop my passport off."* Upon learning this, I felt compelled to seek his assistance. I expressed my request to have my passport dropped off at a specific location, where a man will pick it up and take it to the Embassy. He said, *"Okay! I can do this for you."* Entrusting him with my passport, I departed from the airport and proceeded to my **NYSC Passing Out Ceremony.**

I didn't know what I had done, but I had this assurance in my heart that he would deliver. I told my friend what I had just done when I got to the parade ground for the passing out ceremony. She was astonished. This is because, in Nigeria, giving such an important document to a stranger is a big no-no. Still, I trusted a stranger because the **Holy Spirit** had asked me to. As I proudly received my certificate

from the **NYSC Local Government Inspector (LGI),** my phone rang, and it was Koko. He had just arrived in Lagos and was with the individual I had asked him to meet. *"I've handed over your passport to him,"* he said. Relieved, I listened as the man on the other end confirmed that he had indeed received my passport and pledged to deliver it to the Embassy on my behalf.

A wave of gratitude washed over me as I realized that, once again, God had intervened on my behalf. Exhausted yet content, I returned home and sank into a deep sleep, a rare luxury amidst the turmoil of recent days. Reflecting on the challenges I had overcome, I marveled at my resilience, knowing that it was through divine guidance that I had persevered.

Good News at Last

Three days later, I received a notification from the **DHL office** informing me that the visa office in **Lagos** had sent my passport, which was now in **Abuja.** Quickly, I prepared myself and headed to the **DHL office.** Following the necessary procedures for pickup, I eagerly opened my passport and found the visa inside. Ordinarily, one would expect smiles, joy, and the feeling to jump up at this moment, but my emotions were numb. I had no feelings. The stress of achieving this drained me of any capacity for excitement. Despite this, I contacted Jay, Dammy, Ray, and Micah to share the news with them.

Still excited, the next day, I received a call from **Benin,** informing me that my brother had caused a huge problem, resulting in my mother's arrest. I was urgently summoned to **Benin** to secure her release. However, with my travel plans scheduled in just four days, I found it impossible to go to **Benin.** How could this be happening? Firmly, I declined their request and explored every alternative avenue

available. Regrettably, there was no one to intervene
on her behalf. The

unfortunate reality
was that I couldn't
come to her rescue,
and she had to
endure a night in
the police station
for a crime she didn't commit. *"Thank you,
Nigeria!"* Though I deeply cared, the risk was too
much for me to undertake.

My friends generously offered me money to
purchase my flight tickets to **Germany.** Grateful for
their support, I found out that with their assistance,
the most achievable option for me was a ticket
with **Ethiopian Airlines.** Though it was the most
economical choice, it meant a longer journey to reach
Germany. Nevertheless, I couldn't be more
thrilled—I was finally going to **Germany!**

I AM MICKY

The Moment

The moment to leave for **Germany** had finally come. I was on my way to **Germany,** and the excitement was real. I stayed at Dammy's house in the last days of my departure from **Abuja** because my apartment felt too lonely. Ray often visited me there, and we ate noodles together, trying to make the last days together memorable. Two days before my departure, I found myself struck by illness. Despite being admitted to the hospital and urged to extend my stay for recovery, I insisted on being discharged as my bags were packed with the help of Dammy and my flight booked. Every moment felt like a countdown to the eagerly anticipated D-day.

Enroute Germany

On October 27, I woke up early, dressed, and headed to the airport. I was boarding my flight, and nothing could stop me; I was determined.

Dammy and I at the Airport

Despite my fears, I kept moving and entered the VIP lounge, where I once worked as a Corper, but now, I was a guest. I was treated to tea and snacks by my previous colleagues. Accompanied by Dammy, I caught wind of the initial boarding announcement. Ordinarily, I'd linger until the final boarding call, but excitement and fear swelled within me. I was too excited to get on board, convinced that my troubles would vanish once I stepped onto that plane.

As I boarded the plane, my heart was beating so fast. Leaving behind my country, home, friends, and family, I was embarking on a journey to a foreign land where I knew no one. The reality of being alone settled in as I bid my final farewell to my friend Dammy instead of my family. Joining the line of passengers boarding the plane, I couldn't help but feel the pain of sadness, knowing that my family couldn't accompany me; quite a sad moment. I finally boarded and was on an international flight for the first time. I settled into my seat, bracing myself for the unknown adventure ahead, took pictures, and made some videos. Then, I heard the announcement echoing through the cabin. *"Don't worry, it wasn't a bad one." Relief! Relief!! Relief!!!* It was the pre-flight announcement. I could finally breathe. The plane soared into the cloud. Germany, here I come!

Navigating My Way to Kassel

When I arrived in Ethiopia, the airline scheduled my connecting flight to Germany for midnight; I was to wait for about 2 hours or more. We boarded pretty late, and I found myself at **Frankfurt Airport** at 6 A.M. Uncertain of my next steps, I contemplated how to reach **Kassel.** With the phone numbers of Precious, my Facebook friend, and

Odi, a student at the **University in Kassel** whom I connected with on Instagram, I decided to reach out for help. I called Precious before calling Odi, telling them I had arrived. Inquiring about the journey to **Kassel** during our conversation, Precious advised me to purchase a train ticket. Following her suggestion, I got a ticket for the regular **Regional Deutsche Bahn (DB)** train, unaware I would later board the **Intercity-Express (ICE)** train instead, mistakenly assuming it was the right choice.

As I settled into the first seat I found, a friendly man approached me, offering chocolate. Surprised by the gesture, I thought, *"These people are friendly here!"* Free chocolate—what a rare treat! But in **Germany,** they say there's nothing genuinely free. I was on the wrong train and in the wrong seat altogether. I was seated in the first-class cabin, and I didn't know. Soon enough, the train control officer made his rounds, politely requesting to see my ticket. I boldly brought out my ticket, only to be told it was wrong. I was meant to board a regional train, and not only that, but I was also occupying a seat in the premium first-class section. Caught off guard, I apologized, explaining that I was new to the area and unaware of the rules.

He said, *"You are supposed to be fined sixty euros for such a mistake."* The shock left me speechless, especially since I only had fifty euros in cash after arriving in **Germany.** I pleaded my case, detailing my financial difficulty to him. After some consideration, he kindly said, *"I will let you pay twenty euros, and I will give you a different ticket."* He did that, and I paid the reduced fee and received my new ticket. I couldn't help but wow at the luxury of the first-class ride. *"C'mon! I enjoyed the first-class ride oo."*

Meeting Odi

Arriving at **Kassel Wilhelmshöhe Bahnhof,** Odi awaited me. The renowned **Hercules monument** stood tall in **Kassel,** a testament to the

city's rich heritage, nestled within the picturesque **Bergpark Wilhelmshöhe**. I later had the chance to visit the monument, and it honestly left me in awe. Well, Odi greeted me warmly, and we went to have my first meal together. We opted for **Döner mit Pommes frites** (doner with fries)—a Turkish-style meal with meat and served with potatoes, vegetables, and sauce. The taste still lingers in my memory to this day. After our meal, Odi inquired about my accommodation plans. I confessed I had nowhere to stay and only had 30 euros left. Without hesitation, he said, *"Okay! I know a hostel that costs about 25 euros a night. I'll take you there,* *and tomorrow, I can reach out to some people to help you find a temporary place."*

That night, I spoke to God again before I slept. When I woke up, I encountered the first person in the hostel, whom I would call my first angel in **Germany.** Her name was Anny. *"Hi,"* she greeted me, *"I'm Anny. I arrived late last night. What's your name?"* I introduced myself, saying, *"I'm Micky. I just got to Germany yesterday."* Anny responded with enthusiasm, *"Oh, wow! I'm heading for breakfast. Why don't you join me? I'll pay for your breakfast, and you can tell me more about yourself."*

"I only had five euros left, and unable to afford even breakfast, I found myself in a tight spot. But as fate would have it, the Holy Spirit seemed to intervene. A kind stranger graciously treated me to my first proper meal in Germany." We started a conversation, and she mentioned she was in **Kassel** for a seminar. She would soon return to **Marburg,** where she lived with her family. She said I could come with her to **Marburg** if I didn't find a place to stay in **Kassel.** I

thanked her for the offer and said, *"If I do not find any place to stay, I will give you a call."* After exchanging contacts, we checked out of the hostel and parted ways.

She guided me to the bus stop, where I would board a bus to the university to complete my admission process. Boarding the bus, I made a mistake—I didn't realize I had to purchase a ticket at the bus entrance. I thought I was to pay when I exited the bus, just as we did in **Nigeria.** Unaware of the protocol, I completed the journey without a ticket. Upon reaching my destination, I approached the driver and said, *"Here is my fee."* He responded, *"You think you are smart? Why didn't you pay at the bus station?"* I answered that I had no idea I had to pay before boarding. He was pissed and said, *"Just keep your money and get down."* I felt very embarrassed and ashamed of my mistake. I thought it would make sense if I could disappear from the bus. But I was later grateful for the five euros as I could buy a new charger with it, considering my phone charger was spoilt.

I AM MICKY

After buying the charger, I went to the university to gather the necessary information for a hostel. Upon arrival, the hostel manager told me I had missed the deadline. Disappointed, I went straight to Odi's hostel to speak to him when I finished from school. We talked briefly, and he told me that he called some people for a temporary place to stay, but none responded positively. Just as the situation seemed bleak, there was a knock on the door. It was a girl, Odi's course mate—Her name was Tonye. She had come for guitar practice with Odi. As they sang and played the guitar, the topic of my accommodation came up, and the girl didn't hesitate to assist me with my situation. She suggested calling her boyfriend, proposing I could stay with them as long as needed.

Moving in with Tonye, I found her to be incredibly lovely. That evening, she invited me to join her at a prayer meeting. Excitedly, I accepted. Together, we drove to the venue, marking my first experience with an underground prayer fellowship. In that intimate setting, we prayed, praised, worshipped, and offered prayers for each other's needs. As the service ended, I joined Tonye back to her place, enjoying a peaceful night's sleep. Tonye was genuinely concerned for me. She asked questions and offered assistance, even when I didn't ask. Utilizing her privilege, she promised to help me unblock my blocked account. *"It was required to unblock the funded account with certain documents before one could assess it, and my documents for that were incomplete.* Tonye helped me solve this issue, offered to find me a place to live, and paid my first-semester fee, allowing me to do my school clearance. I couldn't do that without receiving the first bank payment. All of this she did willingly and with the kindness of her heart, proving to be nothing short of an angel.

Finally, I was settling in after paying the semester fee. The first money from the block account was coming, but I had no official address in **Germany.** During my university clearance, I met some fellow students, including KK, who introduced me to a Cameroonian woman offering rental accommodation. Since I had missed the deadline for securing a hostel space at the university, I was exploring alternative options. I contacted the Cameroonian woman, and we scheduled a visit to the property. Accompanied by Tonye, we inspected the place, which unfortunately did not meet our expectations. Tonye sensed that dealing with the woman might be challenging. As we departed, Tonye cautioned me against renting the apartment, advising me to seek alternative arrangements. I heeded her advice and decided to cancel the rental agreement. The woman offered me another deal without relenting, but I won't mention it here for privacy's sake. *"No African should ever take advantage of another African, especially in a foreign country."*

I finally got an address and temporary accommodation at a hostel. Scheduled to move out of Tonye's house, I arranged to have dinner with Anny the evening before. *"Yes, my first angel returned to **Kassel** to check on me."* We had an evening meal together, which would be the last time I saw her to this day.

CHAPTER SEVEN

PEOPLE AND PURPOSE

I FOUND A church to attend—a branch of the Redeemed Christian Church of God in **Kassel.** This church was the same one I had worshipped with in **Nigeria.** As I didn't want to spend my Sundays alone, I went to church every Sunday and attended school on weekdays. However, I soon realized I didn't have suitable winter shoes for school and church, and I couldn't afford a new pair since I was working on a budget. Every day on my way to school, I searched shops for a pair of shoes within my budget. However, the one I liked was above my budget—the price was 23 euros, but I only had 13 euros to spare.

After activating my block account with Tonye's help, I received my first monthly payment and divided the funds into three parts. I sent a part back to **Nigeria** to service my debts, and another part was refunded to Tonye for my semester fee, leaving me with only 20% of the total money to survive on and figure out how to buy a new shoe. Despite this, I still sent money to my family whenever possible while eagerly awaiting the next month's payment. I regularly passed by the shoe shop for two weeks, hoping for a price reduction. Finally, my patience paid off when I discovered the shoe was on sale— selling for 13 euros. I joyfully and excitedly bought my first pair of winter shoes from **Deichmann.**

Moving Out

University life was going great, and I was getting to meet and know many new faces. However, I didn't enjoy some topics in my enrolled course as they didn't resonate with me. Doubts crept in, and at some point, I questioned if I had chosen the right path. I firmly believed I had made a mistake because I didn't directly pick the course of study myself. So, I thought maybe I could switch to something more interesting.

I AM MICKY

Two months later, the owner of the temporary hostel where I stayed was to return, leaving me needing a new place. Yet again, I went to talk to KK, a coursemate and fellow hostel resident. When I told him about my predicament, he mentioned that his cousins had recently rented a house in a village near **Kassel.** I could move in with them for a reasonable fee, which suited my budget perfectly. Without hesitation, I agreed to the offer.

Another Favour

I arrived in **Niestetal,** where four young men were living, and I joined them, making us a group of five. I shared a room with one of them, which made it my new home where I experienced and celebrated my first Christmas in **Germany.** However, the month before Christmas brought some financial stress, as my baby sister got admitted to the university to study nursing, which required a lot of money. I couldn't afford it then due to the multiple loans I was servicing.

In that tight spot, I contacted my friend Naomi in Nigeria; she had previously lent me some money to support my traveling. I asked if I could delay her payment, explaining the urgent need to cover my sister's school fees at that time. Her response stunned me: *"Use the money you owe me to pay for her fees, Micky. Consider it a gift."* I couldn't believe my luck! It was the best gift I could have received, significantly easing my financial burden. With my sister now a university student, I felt immense pride and relief.

Meeting Kelvin and My Plan to Actively Serve God

During Christmas, my roommate and I attended the Redeemed Christian Church of God, which hosted a Christmas party every season. Unfortunately, we arrived late and discovered that members who arrived at church earlier had already consumed all the food, leaving us disappointed and hungry. Suddenly, a guy approached us from behind, remarking, *"You're here late, and all the food is gone.*" We shared a laugh and introduced ourselves; his name was Kelvin. Despite the food scarcity, we gathered what was left and conversed about life and its happenings. Surprisingly, as we ate, we connected immediately, discussing as if we had known each other. As our interaction came to an end, we exchanged phone numbers. To my surprise, Kelvin hails from the same state in **Nigeria** as I did and was also a student at the **University of Kassel.** From that day forward, we became great friends.

We shared information about job possibilities and went to **AIDL** every day after school to buy bread—we were two broke lads managing life. **AIDL** bread became our daily food, considering it was cheap—only 0.15 cents each. This cheese-flavored bread nourished our souls as we would always eat it every day after classes with smiles in our eyes, grateful for something to fill our stomachs.

Despite sharing a room with my roommates, we attended different churches. One of my roommates, Eazy, invited me to his church one day, stating that it was a different atmosphere, and I decided to visit. That's where I first met Pastor Steve and his wife. The atmosphere in their church was unlike anything I had experienced before; I felt a sense of peace and belonging that I hadn't felt in a long time. There and then, I decided to continue attending.

Pastor Steve's wife was genuinely caring towards the congregation. She'd often call me to check in and see how I was doing. During one of the church services, Pastor Steve asked for volunteers to lead the IT Department. When no one stepped forward, he inquired, *"Who here knows about computer programs?"* A few hands, including mine, shot up. Without hesitation, he chose me for the role. While I had been an active church member in the past, primarily because of my mother, this time, I decided to do something for God and the church community wholeheartedly. Sitting before the computer, I whispered, *"God, I'm ready to work for you. Please, work for me too."* Life wasn't easy, and I wasn't living in the best conditions. That was my prayer request at the start of January 2019. I remember playing the song—*He Made a Way* by Travis every day as I walked through the streets of **Germany** and went to class, seeking solace in its comforting melody.

Meeting Rene

One evening in February 2019, while chatting with my roommate, Eazy, I also talked to a friend on Facebook. She inquired about how I made my hair in **Germany,** to which I responded that I hadn't found anyone to do it for me yet. She suggested I join an online platform to connect with **Africans** in the area. Taking her advice, I downloaded an online App that evening and connected with a girl, though our interactions were infrequent.

Then, one day after school, I received a consistent alert from the App. Opening the App and assuming it was the girl, I was only surprised to find out it was someone else named Rene, a German. We got talking, and I was impressed by his excellent command of English. He expressed a desire for friendship as we chatted. I discovered he was a former student at the **University of Kassel,** and in my unbelief, I found it hard to believe he was genuinely German due to his excellent English. So, I voiced my concern, suggesting he might be a *scammer.* He reassured me of his authenticity and said, *"Give me your number, and I'll call you."* I gave him my number; as promised, he called me on a video call to confirm his realness. I was pleasantly surprised to find that he was indeed genuine.

Rene offered to meet me in person, and I agreed. We decided to meet at a bar in **Kassel**. *"Remember, I don't drink due to my alcohol intolerance."* We both ordered non-alcoholic drinks. However, when the drinks arrived, I realized I had ordered the wrong drink, and I didn't like it—it tasted weird. This error was because I couldn't understand the language in which the menu was written, considering I was new in **Germany.** Noticing my reaction, Rene offered to exchange his drink with mine, which he did, and it was much better. We both laughed about the mix-up.

I learned he had recently visited **Nigeria** and stayed there for three months. As we talked, he spoke about his recent breakup with his **Nigerian** partner, revealing that he was heartbroken. I gave him words of hope and explained that life can sometimes be unfair. I told him I could be his friend and that he could talk to me anytime; we both lifted each other's spirits. I shared my frustration about the delay in receiving my **German tax number,** which resulted in me being unable to work for three months after my arrival. However, I received it a week ago and informed him I was now open to finding a job.

Finding A Job and Rene's Interest

To my surprise, Rene offered to assist me in finding a job. Doubtful, I mentioned that we had barely met, but he reassured me, dismissing my concerns and suggesting we check out a few places he knew. That evening, Rene drove us around searching for job opportunities, and we chatted as Rene moved. After several unsuccessful attempts, it was getting late when he kindly offered to drop me off at home, which I agreed to. As we approached my house, he said, *"I believe I've found a wife."* I responded that I wasn't looking for a husband, and we laughed about it before he dropped me off.

When I entered the house, I told my roommate about Rene before heading to bed. That night, I had my first dream in **Germany,** sparking a series of other dreams that turned me into a dreamer. In this dream, I saw Rene. He sat before me, watching over me as I slept like a guardian. Upon waking, I couldn't comprehend the significance of the dream. Honestly, if I am being honest, what is he protecting me from?

Love Interest and Rejection

On the other hand, my roommate Eazy suddenly started developing a love interest in me. Regardless of my consistent explanations that

I wasn't interested in dating anyone, he kept trying to persuade me to date him. However, my rejection only seemed to fuel his jealousy, especially towards my new friend, Rene. He outrightly told me that I didn't give him a chance because I wanted to date this white man. *"That was a racist thing to say. Yes!! Black people can be racist, too."*

Despite my assurances that I wasn't romantically involved with Rene, my roommate remained unconvinced. Later, the situation got out of control when they invited Rene as a guest to a party in **Kassel.** The crowd warmly received him; his easygoing nature and love for dancing won over everyone. Frustrated and filled with anger, my roommate left the party early that night.

When I got home that night, Eazy confronted me, revealing his pent-up frustrations. He reminded me that he had allowed me to stay in the house rent-free for two months, even though I insisted on paying half of the rent. His only condition was that I dated him—a condition I had firmly rejected. He insisted that if my answer remained unchanged, I would have to vacate the premises immediately. Facing an order to move out of the hostel at midnight shocked and confused me.

Despite my efforts to plead with him, his reaction left me feeling frightened and uncertain. Turning to our other roommates for support, I hoped they could intervene and calm him down. Unfortunately, he remained firm in his demand that I leave. It was a painful situation I had never imagined I would find myself in.

"Who should I call?" It was already late. Then, I considered that Rene might still be awake. I dialed his number, and thankfully, he answered promptly. *"Hey Rene, could you possibly pick me up tonight? I find myself without a place to stay."* He assured me he'd be there in 20 minutes. Quickly, I gathered my belongings and waited for him. True to his word, he arrived right on time. Immediately, he pulled up, helped me load all my luggage into his car, and we set off.

Moving in with Rene

Arriving at his home, he offered me his room to sleep in while he settled in the living room, encouraging me to feel at ease. He added, *"I'll respect your space and won't come close to you if you're uncomfortable."* I opted to stay in the living room, and that night, tears streamed down my face as I cried myself to sleep. I could not explain the pain I felt. *"I need a place at the university hostel,"* I whispered in a short prayer. *"Please, God, help me."*

A week later, after moving in with Rene, I received an email from the **student service office** offering me a spot in the hostel. Excitedly, I told Rene about it, expressing my intention to find a job and move out to give him some space. He responded, *"Fine, if that's what you want."* I clarified, *"Yes, I want to move out, but I haven't found a job yet, and I still can't afford any rent."*

With a remaining debt of about one thousand eight hundred euros, I reluctantly declined the hostel offer, choosing to stay at Rene's place. We continued our friendship and attended church together every Sunday. Meeting with Pastor Steve, Rene struck up a friendship with him, and they bonded over shared humor during every Nigerian church service. Two

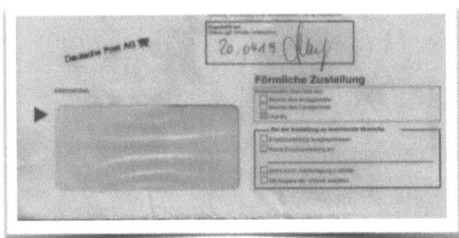

months later, I received my first **red letter** from Germany.

A Supposed Scam and a Second Chance

A fellow Nigerian student called me and asked, *"Did you receive any letter from the university?"* I replied, *"No, I haven't. What letter are you referring to?"* She tried to explain that the university had discovered something—a discovery regarding a supposed scam where individuals had submitted fraudulent results to gain admission. *"But why should I be concerned about that?"* I inquired. She said, *"You might be affected since we all used the same admission agent."* I acknowledged that we had indeed used the same agent. However, I remained uncertain about being affected, as I had submitted my original documents to the agent and graduated with a **1.4 GPA (German grade)**. *"Well, if you didn't receive the letter, you're lucky,"* she remarked.

While trying to understand what she meant, the letter arrived in my postbox the following day. Oops! The tension was unbearable. It was a red letter, which I showed to Rene. He urged, *"Open it. This seems urgent, and you must respond to it."* So, with fear, I tore it open, only to be met with the biggest shock of my life. I was about to lose admission if I failed to submit my official original documents and transcript to the university within 14 days.

I began panicking excessively, overwhelmed by fear. *"How could this even happen?" "I've done nothing wrong,"* I reassured Rene. *"I couldn't have committed something terrible. I submitted all the required documents to the agent and the Embassy. Wouldn't they have detected any fraud? Why would they offer me the visa if it was fraudulent?"* These and many more questions raced through my mind. I was on the verge of losing the primary purpose that brought me to **Germany** in 14 days. What can I do?

I called the **Nigerian** student back, assuring her that I had received the letter today and confirming that I had done nothing wrong. She revealed that five other people were involved and that they had planned to run from **Kassel.** She also mentioned that I could explore different options: fleeing **Germany** or distancing myself from the university to accept Rene's marriage proposal. It seemed like a way out, a solution that would save me from running, but deep down, I knew it would compromise my integrity and make me feel deceitful. It would mean giving up on my chance to defend myself and forfeiting the opportunity to earn a master's degree from **Germany**—a great country. Faced with these choices, I decided to stay and fight back, as I always loved a good challenge.

Remembering the biblical adage, *"And ye shall know the truth, and the truth shall make you free,"* I found solace in confronting the situation head-on. Understanding the gravity of the situation, Rene pledged his support, insisting he would accompany me to the university. Determined, I drafted a response to the letter via email, preparing myself for the challenges ahead.

The Search for My Originals and A Switch of Course

Rene and I headed to the university together. Upon arrival, we realized we needed an appointment but had none. Luckily, Rene leveraged his status as a citizen to secure an audience with Frau Clara. She welcomed us into her office, and we took our seats. Rene took the lead, speaking on my behalf as if he were my spokesperson. Frau Clara believed I hadn't committed any wrongdoing but required evidence to support my innocence. Surprisingly, she showed me a forged certificate that closely resembled the original, which was not mine. Determined to clear up the mess, I told her, *"I will get you the original documents."* She responded by giving me a deadline, stating, *"I will give you some more time."*

I finally obtained my original certificates by contacting my alma mater, **the University of Benin,** in **Nigeria.** I requested that they send my original university transcript and statement of results via post. However, as time passed, without their arrival, Frau Clara notified me that the application deadline was close. I contacted the university again, and they said they had sent it. In the meantime, I attempted to present my student copy to Frau Clara's office, awaiting the arrival of the official documents. To my surprise, Frau Clara wrote to inform me that someone had told the university that my transcript had been delivered to a different office, prompting them to redirect it to her. Upon receiving them, Frau Clara asked, *"What are your intentions now? Your actual results are better than the fake ones. You graduated with an excellent grade."* I replied, *"I intend to continue my studies here but in a different course. I want to switch courses."* *"In that case, you'll need to apply for the new course,"* she advised. *"The application deadline is fast approaching. I'll personally speak to the heads of other departments on your behalf, so you can submit your application promptly."* Grateful for her assistance, I thanked her and departed. This opportunity marked a second chance for me at the university. *"Now, I must prove myself and secure my admission anew. However, this time, I am doing it on my own, and with my authentic certificates."*

The Process of Gaining Another Admission

In preparation, I began legitimizing my certificates to send them to **Uni-Assist**, an academic body supporting admission processes and certificate evaluation in **Germany.** That morning, Rene and I hurried to the **Government Legitimation Office**, considering we had a deadline. It was there I would have my first racist experience. Upon entering the office, the man blatantly ignored me. Despite our wait, he continued to disregard my presence. Frustrated, I approached him and said, *"You have called everyone here, even those who arrived after me, yet I am still waiting. Is there any problem?"* His response was shocking: *"I will not touch your documents or attend to you."* Confused, I asked, *"Why, if I may ask?"* He responded, *"Because you don't deserve it."*

Original

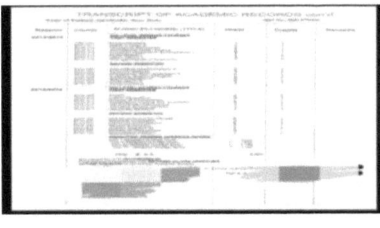

Fake

Feeling upset, I went to Rene and told him about what had occurred. Rene's reaction was immediate and intense—he was furious. He instructed me to wait in the car while he handled the situation. Without hesitation, I complied. Rene went into the office and confronted the man, his anger evident. *"You are a racist, and I will make you a popular one. I am a registered journalist who would put you on the papers,"* Rene threatened. The man, clearly scared, began to plead for mercy. *"Please ask her to come back with the documents. I will sign them,"* he said.

Upon receiving Rene's call, I returned to find the situation under control. The man, now composed, apologized for his rude behavior. I could focus and complete my task on time with the matter resolved. I promptly sent the required documents to the **Uni-Assist,** and they arrived on time, and I was swiftly evaluated and approved. I then forwarded this approval to the **University in Kassel.** However, this time, the branch was located in **Witzenhausen (the cherry town)**, a city in the **Werra-Meißner-Kreis**

 district **North of Hessen, Germany.** Witzenhausen has gained national recognition for creating the **Biotonne,** a container for biological waste. It is also renowned as a significant **cherry-growing region.** In my almost six years in **Germany,** I have never tasted cherries as sweet as those from **Witzenhausen.** Annually, the city hosts the **Kesperkirmes,** also known as the *"Cherry Fair,"* where a **Cherry Queen (Kirschenkönigin)** is selected and crowned.

The **University of Kasel** has a satellite campus in **Witzenhausen,** which offers programs focused on **ecological agricultural sciences.**

This factor makes **Witzenhausen** one of the smallest university towns in **Germany.** Like my undergraduate experience, I have been redirected to a small sub-campus again.

I AM MICKY

To my delight, the university offered me an admission, and the admissions board was impressed with my application. When I received the email

University of Kassel - Witzenhausen

confirming my new acceptance, I couldn't contain my excitement—I jumped and danced for joy.

Once again, I am a student pursuing a course I love. What a testimony! This admission would not have been possible without Rene's unwavering help and support. As I reflected on this journey, I flashed back to my dream. This fulfillment was one of the protections God told me about in the dream.

I began preparing for my new campus by visiting two months earlier to familiarize myself with the surroundings. While exploring, Rene and I shared a meal at **Mensa** (a subsidized student restaurant). At one point, amidst our conversation, Rene jokingly remarked, *"We should get married. I don't want to*

147

lose you to these students here. " We both laughed at his funny comment.

The Marriage

In August 2019, we tied the knot in **Denmark.** Pastor Steve and his wife, who had become like parents to me,

graced our wedding with their presence. They were our pillars, the ones who turned to in times of joy and sorrow. Rene and I decided to

have a very small wedding and planned for a bigger celebration later. After the wedding, we started various side hustles while I was job hunting. Fortunately, Rene landed a new job while I secured a student job cleaning at a local supermarket.

School had resumed and I was doing great. I was fortunate to have crossed paths with amazing people such as Marshia, Sharon, CJ, Eunice, Funke, Jenifer, Danny, Dayo, Joseph, Emelda and Michael. We shared laughter, ate at the **University Mensa,** and created lasting memories.

Shortly after, Rene was admitted to a short course at the university to study **International Project Management** organized by **Gesellschaft**

für Nachhaltige Entwicklung (GNE), which allowed us precious moments together during breaks.

CHAPTER EIGHT

THE BUBBLE

STRENGTH ISN'T ABOUT never feeling tired, in pain, or having doubts; it's about finding the will to keep moving. At this point, I had endured so much pain, holding onto strength for too long without giving myself the space to process everything. I was forced into adulthood way too early, carrying the pain and hurt of navigating life alone. I was living in a bubble that felt ready to burst.

One morning, around 5 AM, thoughts of my friend Ray filled my mind before I headed to school. We hadn't spoken in a while, and I was eager to update him on my progress and how I was settling into **Germany.** Knowing how much he cared for me, it was fair to reach out. So, at 6 AM, I sent him a message with a smiling sticker, eager to reconnect. He saw the message and replied with a sticker of his own. Determined to call him after my classes, I left for school.

I AM MICKY

"I write this part with tears in my eyes." My emotions took a sudden turn while I was in class. Around 5 PM, I received a message from an old neighbour who knew Ray. With trembling hands, I picked up my phone and read the shocking news, *"Micky, Ray passed away this morning. He collapsed after returning from the mosque."* Shock and disbelief washed over me as the reality of his death sank in. My dear friend Ray was gone. It seemed impossible. I would never get to speak to him again.

I rose from my seat in the class, my heart bursting with so much pain. Danny, one of my coursemates, noticed my distress and asked what was wrong. I told her I had just lost a dear friend. Seeking some privacy, I withdrew to the restroom, where I wept until I had no tears left. The bubble had burst, and I was completely breaking down.

Returning to class, I quickly gathered my belongings and headed home. Once there, I locked myself in my room and continued to mourn. Memories of our time together in Abuja flooded my mind. Ray had been more than a friend; he was like a brother. He believed in my potential, often saying I would be a wealthy woman while foreseeing a prosperous future. As I left Nigeria, his parting words echoed, *"Don't leave me here alone, lonely." "Yet, that's what I had done, and the guilt was overwhelming."* My mind raced with unanswered questions. *"Why hadn't I reached out to Ray sooner? Could a call that morning have made a difference?"* These thoughts weighed heavily on me, clouding my judgment and deepening my sorrow, putting me in a place of confusion and pain. Depression slowly crept in, draining my energy and leaving me utterly exhausted.

When I shared the news of Ray's passing with Rene, my husband, he struggled to understand the depth of my grief. The pain was immense—not only had I lost a friend, but also a brother, a mentor, and an inspiration in countless ways that no one else had ever been in my life. While in my grief, I held to a silent hope that someday, I would offer his daughter the same guidance and support her father gave me, keeping his memory alive through my actions.

The Wave of COVID-19

Every day, I merely survived, feeling like I wasn't living. Broken inside, I found it hard to navigate through each moment. The stress was intense, and an examination was coming up. I woke up one morning to a ringing in my ears—tinnitus triggered due to the stress. Faced with no other choice, I had to cancel my examination. Then, amidst this miserable reality, the **COVID-19 virus** struck, changing everything. Classes shifted online, and I felt myself losing the only community I had outside the confines of my home.

As I struggled to balance my cleaning job, online classes, family responsibilities, loan repayments, driving license preparations, and the heavy grief of losing a close friend and brother, my husband Rene was making plans to sell our house. The pressure seemed to isolate me further, challenging my capacity to cope.

I AM MICKY

I deactivated and deleted my Facebook account and changed my Instagram profile—deleting most photos and turning off the comment section. I was going through a tough time, and the struggle was real. We were so close to selling our house in **Hessen,** a challenge I couldn't bring myself to object. Just as we found a buyer and were about to finalize the sale, my husband and I discovered we had contracted the **COVID-19 virus.** The severity of our symptoms was so much that we thought we would die. This devastating news, however, spared us from having to sell the house. What a relief! While dealing with grief and illness, we found consolation in being spared the ordeal of moving.

Based on my personal experience, I'd like to share some signs that may indicate your friend or family member might be having a tough time mentally or potentially facing depression:

I. Excessive Sleeping — Changes in sleep patterns, such as always wanting to sleep or sleeping more than usual.

II. Loss of Interest — Losing interest in activities they once loved. For example, I used to enjoy surfing the internet but eventually needed to avoid social media.

III. Anxiety

IV. Distancing (Social Withdrawal) — Wanting to avoid contact with others, like my coursemates.

V. Numbness — It felt like I had no feelings, sympathy, or empathy anymore.

The Cryptocurrency Bull Run

I continued with school, spending most of my time glued to my computer screen as all classes had moved online. My schoolmates rarely visited, caught up in their busy schedules and personal hustles. Reflecting on this, I realized we all faced different challenges. Though I wished for more support from them, I understood the demands they faced.

Meanwhile, amidst these challenges, I remembered it was the year for another

cryptocurrency bull run. As I struggled mentally and health-wise, I decided to quit my cleaning job to focus on completing my Master's without taking a break from school. This option left me mostly at home while my husband went to work. Seeing I had no source of income anymore, I went to my room, looked up at the pictures of my siblings and me, and tried to talk to God. *"Hey God, I quit my job and can no longer help my siblings continue their education. Please, help me. I also need someone I could open up to."* I said, tears streaming down my face.

During this period, I found comfort in joining various Telegram groups and seeking insights and opportunities in the **crypto market.** Although I rarely spoke to Kelvin out of respect for my marital commitment, our paths crossed again, which led to discussing potential investment opportunities for the upcoming **crypto bull run.** My primary concern was securing funds to support my siblings.

Together, Kelvin and I decided to invest in **Dogecoin.** Excited by the prospects, I shared the idea with my husband upon his return from work. Without hesitation, he opened his first **crypto account** on the **Binance App,** and together, we ventured into the world of cryptocurrency investment. While I had invested in crypto before, this time, it felt different as I embarked on this journey alongside my life partner.

The investment in **Dogecoin** prospered, and surprisingly, at the same time, God answered my short and direct prayer for help due to my lack of a job. Back in **Nigeria,** my baby brother had applied for a scholarship without my knowledge. He wasn't sure he would get it. However, somehow, my brother got a fully funded scholarship to a private university. Joy filled my heart again as he shared this information with me. *"God is truly the present help in times of need."*

Meeting Sunshine (Buky)

One day, I joined a voice seminar on Telegram, where the topic revolved around the **cryptocurrency market** and its future opportunities. During the conversation, a woman's captivating voice struck me. Her eloquence resonated with me, reminding me of myself. After the seminar, I decided to send her a private message expressing my admiration for her contributions. She graciously responded with a simple *"Thank you."* Encouraged by her response, I introduced myself, revealing that I was Micky from **Germany** and that it was a pleasure to meet her. In return, she told me her name was Sunshine (Buky) and mentioned her strong Christian faith—she loved God deeply.

We took our relationship further as we started to communicate more. Our conversations were not only centered on **cryptocurrency** but also on our relationship with God and our families. As our discussions progressed, I gradually opened up to her, sharing my struggles and the pain of losing my dear

159

friend—Sunshine was a prayer answered. To my relief, Sunshine proved to be a compassionate listener. She offered wise counsel while attentively absorbing my words. Her genuine presence and help became a source of comfort during those challenging times. Sunshine's unwavering support truly meant the world to me.

Family Reconnection and Investment

After eight years of no contact, my father finally reconnected with the family. That year, I had my first conversation on the phone with him. As we spoke, my heart was racing so fast it felt like I was having a heart attack—a replay of how I felt when he sent the text message asking us to survive any way we could without him. I told Sunshine again about my struggle to reconnect with him, and she advised me to take my time and approach the situation slowly. Our chats became a daily habit, and one day, she called to tell me about a coin called **Moon,** urging me to invest in it. I agreed, and when my husband returned from work, I told him, and he, too, invested

300 euros. To our amazement, the 300 euros turned into an unbelievable amount within two weeks. We were shocked and overly excited. Sunshine also invested, and her investment saw exponential growth. My husband was astonished, remarking that no woman had ever helped him make such a significant sum. This action was how Sunshine changed my mental and financial life—she truly lived up to her name as she was indeed a sunshine.

As my situation and health improved, I started to plan my journey to **Nigeria** to visit my family and friends like Sunshine and to undertake research for my **Master's thesis.** It would be my first trip home in three years—a journey to reunite with my family and seek closure for the death of my friend Ray.

The Encounter

Sunshine often shared her Bible meetings with me as I frequently talked to God and played songs that uplifted my spirit. One day, on September

17, 2021, I encountered the Holy Spirit in the most powerful way. A strange feeling came over me as I washed the dishes and sang. I broke down in tears and began speaking in tongues, uttering words whose meanings I did not understand. I was moved from one area of my house to another, grateful to be alone. *"If my husband had been home, he might have thought I was losing my mind."* This encounter lasted for nearly 30 minutes. The Holy Spirit passed a message to me, and I prayed fervently against an accident. However, I didn't know for whom. When the experience was over, I immediately called my baby brother Jemie, who was practising for his driver's license. I feared the accident might involve him, so I advised him to be cautious while learning. I returned to the dishes and replayed the song once more. I thought the spirit would come upon me the second time to reveal who he was talking about, but he didn't return. It seemed like he had finished passing his message. I kept the experience to myself as I planned my trip to **Nigeria.**

My Trip to Nigeria

I had a ticket for October 25, 2021. I arrived in **Lagos, Nigeria,** with my Pastor's wife. Upon arrival, I fell ill and was diagnosed with malaria. Two

days later, I felt a bit better and travelled to **Abuja** to commence my research with the **National Agency for Food and Drug Administration and Control (NAFDAC),** the **Standards Organization of Nigeria (SON),** and

several other **food companies.** *While in Abuja, the strangest thing happened, which I have chosen not to discuss in this book.*

I AM MICKY

I travelled to **Benin** to visit my family, and my illness worsened during my stay there, leaving me sick throughout my time in **Nigeria.** Desperate to return to **Germany,** I felt shattered by the memories and trauma **Benin** stirred up, prompting my departure. I left for **Lagos,** this time to see Sunshine, a woman with a lot of grace, and we had a fun time together. Two days later, despite my condition, I departed for **Germany.** The thought of possibly dying in **Nigeria** weighed heavily on me, especially as I bid farewell to my mother and friends at the airport, filled with sorrow at leaving them again. We boarded the plane, and right there on the plane, I wept and groaned, feeling utterly lost. The tears continued until I landed in **Germany,** where my husband awaited me at the airport, ready to take me home. My husband saw the sadness in my eyes after my return from **Nigeria**. He promised to invite my mother to spend time with me.

Master's Defense

The anticipation of my mother's coming gave me joy, as it meant I would no longer be lonely in the house when my husband went to work. I joyfully continued investing in **cryptocurrency** and enjoyed every opportunity during the bull run. We purchased a new home before I travelled to **Nigeria.** That way, we were busy renovating the house in preparation for tenants to rent the place. Everything was improving for me mentally, especially with the hope of my mother coming to **Germany.**

Early in 2022, I successfully defended my **Master's thesis** and officially became a **Master's graduate,** earning an **A.** Despite desiring more, I acknowledged the challenges I had overcome to reach that point in my academic journey. Achieving an **A+** or **A-** didn't hold the same significance for me anymore, given the many **A's** I had accumulated throughout my educational journey and the fact that I could have died while in **Nigeria—**

life and health were now important to me. Notably, the only exam I ever failed was **Chemistry.** Regardless, I was now a graduate, fulfilling my dream of attaining a **Master's degree.**

Still basking in the euphoria of being the latest graduate, my husband sent the invitation to my mother, but she hesitated to come, which made me feel more disappointed. I tried to convince her, but she had several reasons for not visiting.

Failed Investment

My husband had invested in the failed **Luna coin,** a meme. I watched his 200 euros grow to 4000 euros, and when I asked him to sell it, he refused. We had a rough conversation, and I went to bed early in anger. I was upset because he said some hurtful words to me. By 11 PM, the coin had crashed, and his 4000 euros were now 200 euros. He came to bed to apologize for not listening to me. Still, the previous conversation had been hurtful, so I didn't care what he said. In the morning, in that sorrowful state, I called my mother on the phone and cried while speaking to her, saying, *"Come to Germany, please. I'm tired of being here alone."* All my life, I've mostly had to take action alone. She felt my pain as a mother can feel a child's pains sometimes, and this time, she put in all the effort to come to visit us.

Mom's Trip to Germany

*I was elated. "My mother was coming to **Germany**!"* It was her first time leaving Nigeria and flying on a plane, and my dream was to give her a great experience. I contacted all my old acquaintances at the airport in **Abuja**. I informed them that my mother would pass through **Abuja International Airport** to **Germany.** I asked them to provide her with the best treatment and access to the **VIP lounge.**

When she landed, I was delighted to hear she had a wonderful time in **Abuja** before continuing her journey to **Germany.** She officially met my husband for the first time since she couldn't attend our wedding then. Luckily, her visit coincided with my husband's birthday, August 19, and our third wedding anniversary, August 20. It was great to have my mother here. I welcomed her in **Frankfurt** with my husband. We greeted her with beautiful flowers and warm hugs. She joined us home, and after settling in, we took her to church, where she met with Pastor Steve and his wife.

We explored nearby cities in Hessen together—watching her enjoy herself gave me so much joy. During her stay in **Germany,** my university sent me my official **Master's certificate** to our house, which I proudly showed her,

and she danced happily. With that joy, I told her, *"I will take you to my university so you can have a feel of what an international university looks like."* We arrived at the **University of Kasel** at

Witzenhausen the following week. We took lovely pictures as my husband told her about the university's history. With a smile, she said, *"I never went to a university, but I am here today at a university in Germany because of my daughter."* She was proud, and I could feel it. *"Most Nigerian parents don't express emotions openly, but I could sense her joy from her words."* She was overjoyed to visit where I completed my studies.

Her Return

As her time in **Germany** ended, she had to return to **Nigeria.** We drove her to the airport and said our goodbyes before returning home. Once she departed, tears welled in my eyes, and I cried. It was back to isolation for me as my husband was always at work. My husband, being an only child with both parents deceased, lacked family members. I must say that staying with my mother was not the easiest, as we still had our unresolved issues. I was still angry with the situation from my childhood; my pain mostly was why she let herself suffer so much, but when she left, I tried to heal from this personally.

A Step to Healing

I was open to working again. I volunteered in an **NGO** partnering with **Deutsches Rotes Kreuz DRK** as a **laboratory assistant**—testing people for **COVID-19.** *"Having experienced COVID, it made sense to do something to help others."* While on break one day, browsing through **TikTok,** I stumbled upon a video recommending a book for individuals struggling with issues stemming from their childhood. The book is titled "**Adult Children of Emotionally Immature Parents** by Lindsay C. Gibson." I went straight to **Amazon** and ordered the book. People's testimonies filled the comment section, describing the impact of the book on their lives. After receiving the book, I took it to work with me every day to read during my break. The book proved to be a source of comfort, reassuring me that the difficult situation of reconnecting with my parents wasn't my fault or that of my siblings. However, the book didn't heal me entirely—I felt triggered whenever I heard about specific issues.

The Accident

Three months after my mother left **Germany,** precisely on October 18, 2022, I experienced a terrible accident. It occurred when I accompanied my husband to the garage to work on his car. However, I decided to run an errand to **Witzenhausen** to buy gas and planned to catch up with a schoolmate, Dayo. As I drove along the road, the steering wheel of my car suddenly seized, leaving me with no control. The car began sliding at a dangerous speed, heading to fall off a bridge. In panic, I cried out the only name I could think of— **Jesus.** Miraculously, I found myself in the bushes, with a large log of wood preventing the car from plunging further. I was shocked and shaken to the core. **Jesus** had intervened and saved my life again. I immediately called my husband, who rushed to my side quickly. This message was the accident the Holy Spirit tried to minister to me during my encounter with him on September 17, 2021. I was very grateful for his mercies. Following the incident, I developed a newfound fear of driving, which persisted for several weeks, leading me to avoid getting behind the wheel altogether.

CHAPTER NINE

CAREER IN GERMANY

UPON EARNING MY Master's degree, I embarked on a journey to find a career that resonated with my passions and qualifications. I obtained an **International Food Business and Consumer Studies** degree from the **University of Kasel** and **Hochschule Fulda.**

My interest and passion for **food safety,** and **quality assurance** are rooted in my childhood. At nine, I first learned about "quality assurance" and immediately understood its primary importance. An unforgettable event during my early years, between the ages of eight and ten, solidified this understanding. I had a favourite drink from a renowned soft drink company. One day, as I eagerly opened a bottle of my favourite flavour from the crates my brother had purchased, I was shocked to find a small cockroach inside it. Confused, I was

173

unsure how this could happen. I asked my elder brother, *"How could this be possible?"* I was told that the person in charge of quality control had failed to remove the **defective samples.** That incident left a lasting impression on me, marking my first encounter with "**quality assurance."**

Take it back to when I was fourteen years of age. We went on a school excursion to visit the company that produced my favourite beverage and its competitors. I was excited to see what goes on where the company made my favourite drink. In front of the **production line,** the **quality assurance manager** educated us on **quality assurance and quality control processes.** While witnessing the thorough inspection process, the **quality controller** seated close to the products looked through them carefully and removed the defective ones. That gave me an insight into the industry's work ethics. I realized that errors could occur due to various factors, such as **inadequate bottle cleaning** or the **absence of a quality controller** during packaging. This experience deepened my understanding of the work system.

God redirected me to study **Home Economics Management and Education** for my bachelor's degree, where my focus shifted toward **safety and nutrition.** My eagerness for **consumer safety** was evident in my project, which attracted the interest of every lecturer in my project work. However, the incident of the fake admission at the **University of Kassel** reawakened my passion for **food safety and consumer studies,** guiding me back to my original path.

Job Search

I casually searched for a job while learning **German**—I focused more on improving my **German language** skills before applying. After crafting a **Curriculum Vitae (CV),** I embarked on the application process and encountered numerous rejections. Disheartened, I returned to the drawing board to reconsider my approach. I attached significant information, such as adding my husband's last name, Schneider, to mine. *"Perhaps,"* I reasoned, *"my previous surname was too challenging for some employers to pronounce."* But even with the seemingly more straightforward name, rejections persisted. Frustrated, I decided to hand over my job search to God. Before my birthday, I made a simple yet earnest request for employment from Him. Meanwhile, I continued volunteering, finding solace in the absence of stress. Although the volunteer role was not in a **food manufacturing company,** I found fulfilment in fully engaging with the company.

An Appeal to Recruiters and Hiring Managers in Germany

I strongly advocate for esteemed recruiters and hiring managers to adopt a more inclusive approach to hiring international students. Acquiring fluency in a new language during one's twenties presents significant challenges, compounded by the diverse obstacles that life often presents during this stage. The international students I have encountered consistently demonstrate exceptional intelligence and an outstanding work ethic. Many embark on their academic journeys in foreign lands, undertaking the challenging task of mastering a new language while simultaneously shouldering responsibilities such as employment to support their education and provide for their families.

*I implore you to extend opportunities to these individuals. While proficiency in **German** is undoubtedly valuable, the presence of candidates distinguished by their outstanding personal qualities and character attributes can prove even more beneficial to your organization.*

The Gateway

After nearly four years without a vacation together, my husband decided it was time for a **getaway.** This was our first time travelling outside of **Germany** for a holiday, primarily due to the constraints of COVID-19 and our limited free time. He wanted to lift my spirits and suggested a trip to **Spain.** As a gesture of kindness, he offered to book our flights, eager to provide me with a much-needed break.

Last Christmas, we encountered a couple that led to unexpected connections. When I needed a new phone after my screen broke twice, we purchased a used iPhone 12 Pro Max from a couple we met on **eBay.** Surprisingly, this transaction blossomed into a friendship, and we bonded with the couple after the business deal. In a twist of fate, I also purchased a car from them. The vehicle caught my eye, and I was eager to make it mine. *"There is another story about this car, but I could tell it when someone wants to hear it."* For now, let's focus on our upcoming trip to **Spain.**

As we prepared for our journey to **Spain**, we needed someone to drop us off at the train station in **Hannover,** where we would board our flight. With few people available to help, the newly acquainted couple kindly offered to drive us to the train station at noon. Arriving at the station, we caught our flight to **Mallorca, Spain,** on March 5, 2023. The excitement of being on a plane again was noticeable, as the last time I flew, I was on my way to **Nigeria** to visit my family.

Loss of Job

When we arrived in **Spain,** I was exhausted. I quickly jumped into bed and slept straight through until the following day. Waking up, I felt so good and refreshed to have taken this break. Three days later, we went for a long walk around **Mallorca,** admiring the beauty of nature.

Coming back very tired, I went straight to bed. Upon waking up, my husband shared an email from our mutual boss that had come in on March 9, 2023. The email revealed that the COVID-19 centre where I volunteered as a **Laboratory Assistant** was shutting down, leaving me jobless. Since I was losing my job, my boss kindly presented alternative employment options. Still, I knew deep down that continuing at the company wasn't where my passion lay.

Losing a job while on holiday is undoubtedly not the best experience. Still, we decided to push forward and make the most of our time away. Amidst the relaxation, I found solace in reading the book **"God and the Big Bang."** Its pages taught me about God, reminding me to seek His presence in the  simplicity of everyday life—in nature, family, and every corner of His existence. It was a gentle reassurance that God was everywhere.

I AM MICKY

The Dream

On March 10, 2023, I had a vivid dream during our holiday. In it, I saw myself surrounded by a sea of **Curricula Vitae** spread across a table, with mine at the bottom of the other piles, which they later moved to the top. When I woke up, I felt uncertain, as if something different would happen. Upon our return to **Germany** on March 12, I wasted no time starting the process. I went into my room, crafted a fresh **Curriculum Vitae,** and transformed my space into a makeshift office, determined to represent the mindset of someone already employed as I had this conviction that I would be getting a job soon. Remember Brown? The girl from camp? I reached out to her as I was drawn to her recent post about God on social media, encouraging me to share insights from a book I had read. Our exchange of experiences and encouragement further solidified my belief in our friendship.

Light At the Tunnel

I resumed my job search and was pleasantly surprised when interview offers started flooding in. I had more interviews than I could handle, leading me to decline some. It shifted from my struggle to secure just one interview to getting many. The first of these interviews took place on March 28, 2023, with Mr. Tom, a recruiter fascinated by my profile. He told me he would schedule three interviews with three companies. I was about to be interviewed for the whole of April. What had started as a quest for just one interview turned into a fully booked month. Remarkably, I passed every first-round interview for each company I was interested in. Subsequently, I found myself in the second round of interviews with five companies simultaneously, each extending an invitation for a physical meeting at their offices.

"Remember the story of Peter, who once went fishing and caught nothing until Jesus instructed him to cast his net again?" That was my present situation. I had fished before but on dry grounds. However, this time,

it was different. I visited three companies and scheduled two more interviews, which I eventually cancelled due to their inability to meet my salary requirements.

As I spoke to my husband about the progress of my interviews with different companies, another company called me. Interestingly, I had applied for the job about a month before through the **University Fulda offline email list.** Initially, I hadn't taken it too seriously, almost forgetting it entirely. Yet, fate intervened when the company unexpectedly contacted me, inquiring if I was available for an interview. Exhausted by prior interviews as I had travelled almost around **Germany,** I hesitated but eventually accepted this one last interview. On the interview day, the recruiter questioned me on a crucial topic concerning **quality management.**
Though my interviews typically took place in **German,** this time, I faced complicated questions that required clear responses. Fearing my limited proficiency in **German** might make me sound unprepared, I opted to answer the questions

in **English.** Mr. Ronny, the interviewer, encouraged me to proceed in English, assuring me, *"It's fine. We understand you."*

A Job Opportunity

This assurance boosted my confidence, and we had the most excellent conversation ever. During the interview, I discovered that the interviewer was a former student of **Fulda University,** the same one I attended. We discussed the possibility of starting as soon as possible. However, the other interviewer suggested that Ronny take some time to cool down, as he appeared to be in a hurry. *"We'll get back to you in two weeks,"* she said, and we bid our farewells.

"I was interested in three companies, whereas five were interested in me, and I had already scheduled one more interview." My next thought was to bring all these companies to God in prayer, as I had no idea which one to say *yes* to. The last companies I had just interviewed with were in the East, and I've never heard enjoyable stories about

the **Eastern region of Germany**. You *can Google this fact if you're interested. "I didn't want to go to the East,"* I told God.

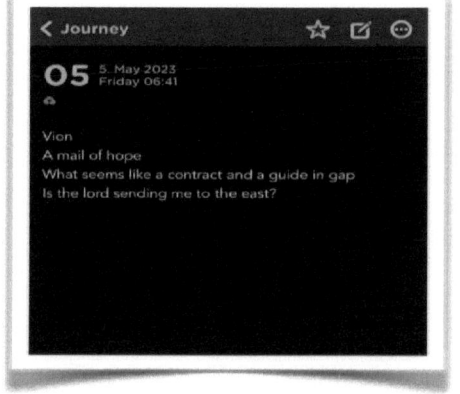

Three days after the interview, I had a dream. I received an email from one of the interviewers, Michaela, the other interviewer. *"Hi Micky, we've decided to move forward with you. Don't worry about a thing. You'll be learning from me, and I'll support you during your time here."* That's what the email said in the dream. When I woke, I exclaimed, *"God, you're sending me East!"* I wrote the dream down in my journey journal.

A few minutes later, I got a call from Michaela, saying, *"I'd like to invite you for a site visit and to meet with the team. What date works for*

you?" She followed up with an email containing the
date and further details of
the company. Again, GOD
DID IT!

CHAPTER TEN

ALTENBURG

IN THE HEART of **Thuringia,** a state in **Central Germany,** lies the picturesque city of **Altenburg.** Here, time stands still amidst its

historic streets, where old buildings stand tall, each bearing the weight of centuries past. Some buildings may appear weathered and worn, their fronts dirtied by time. Yet, within every corner, crack, and broken stone lies a story waiting to be discovered. **Altenburg** belongs to the **Eastern** part of **Germany.**

Although I first heard of this place during my  interview, I only gained more insight into the city when the train stopped at the station. Walking through the town, I felt a connection. It was as if the city represented my life—me standing tall, bearing every weight from my past, with brokenness yet a story waiting to be discovered.

I had never felt more peaceful than when I visited **Altenburg**. No city had ever captured my attention throughout my interviews as it did. While taking a bus to the company, I knew I would be 20 minutes late due to the train delay, typical of the **German railway system.** So, I called Micheala to inform her. Upon arrival, I found her waiting for me. *"Good morning,"* she said at the entrance of the company. *"Can I call you Micky?"* *"Yes, of course",* I responded. *"That's what I'm called."* Later that day, I told her I loved the city, and she was surprised I had said that. She replied, *"Yes, it is a beautiful city."* I did not see the broken buildings or boredom other people saw. Instead, I saw **beauty.**

Michaela and I went upstairs, where she gave me clothes to change into before we headed to the production unit. She showed me around and explained the entire process. Afterward, Michaela took me to an office. *"This could be your office if you decide to take the job, though it's not in the best condition,"* she said.

I didn't mind the office's appearance at that moment. All I felt was a sense of peace, and that was all that mattered. We chatted as we left the office like we'd known each other for ages. I asked about the size of the quality management team. Michaela replied, *"It's just you and me. We'll work closely together, and I'll teach you everything you need to know. You don't have to worry."* This statement confirmed the dream—the email I had read. I felt relieved and told Michaela that my **German** wasn't the best. She replied that her **English** wasn't good either, but she was sure we could do it. After that statement from her, my confidence grew from 70% to 100%.

I went into the conference room to speak to **Human Resources.** While Michaela and I waited, we continued talking, which led to a great conversation. It didn't feel like an interview; it felt like a chat between friends. As we spoke, **Human Resources** seemed impressed with me. We negotiated, and although they asked me to accept a slightly lower salary, I agreed. I left the meeting feeling confident that I had found the best place to work, just as I had requested from God. *"I wanted a workplace that would give me peace of mind. Life can be good without God, but with God, life will be better."* I received the official offer and was ready to move to Altenburg.

I AM MICKY

Moving To Altenburg

I was moving again, as this was my reality. I was scared and not far from anxiety. I had just recovered from several traumas, and I knew that I would be leaving my only family and comfort back in **Hessen.** Starting a new life alone in **Altenburg** meant leaving behind the comforts of my 200-square-meter house with its nice indoor gym and easy access to nature, including a beautiful garden. I was leaving my church, Pastor Steve and his wife, and my home of four years. Yet, I knew I was going to a place God sent me. I believed He would compensate me for my stress.

Before arriving in **Altenburg,** I had contacted several people, telling them I was searching for a place to rent. The night before our departure, a woman uploaded a new flat on **eBay Kleinanzeigen** (classified ads). Upon our arrival in **Altenburg** on June 13, 2023, my husband and I strolled through the city, took in the sights, and visited the **Brüderkirche** (Brethren Church), where we offered our prayers. I prayed to *find purpose,* which I wrote down and placed in the prayer tree. As we continued exploring the city, we were captivated by its charm.

Later, my husband stumbled upon a newspaper containing an advertisement

for a house in the nearby area. I asked him to call about the house and help me contact the woman from **eBay** **regarding** the new flat for rent. He promptly made the calls, and we arranged a visit to the flat for the following day. When we arrived, Oma (grandma) opened the door. We were ten minutes early for the visit. She asked us to look at the flat, which we did, and we liked it. She questioned why I was leaving **Kassel (Grossalmerode)** for **Altenburg** with a grave face.

I tried to answer, but she wasn't impressed. She asked, *"You are leaving your husband in Kassel to work here?"* I replied, *"Yes. I didn't get a chance in Kassel, but I did get a chance here and I want to take it."* She looked a bit disappointed. With her reaction, I did not know if I would get the flat. Before we left, my husband noticed that she was a bit cranky and decided to lighten up the room by talking about her faith, seeing that she was wearing a cross. He asked her, *"Are you a Christian?"* She replied, *"Yes, I am. I go to church."* He wondered if she was Catholic, but she said, *"No, I am not Catholic. I go to the **Brüderkirche (Brethren Church)**, and I am the key holder for the church in **Altenburg**."* That's when we told her that we are also members of the **Brüderkirche** in **Kassel,** and it was nice to know that she was a fellow Christian.

She told us she needed time to think and decide who to give the flat to. Silently, I prayed to

God, *"God, I want this flat, and I will get it."* One week later, my husband called her, and she said she had not decided yet. Two days later, she contacted him herself and said, *"Tell your wife to come take the flat. I want her to meet my daughter."* Excitedly, I went to the flat, and she smiled so much this time. It was like I was meeting a different person. Something about her had changed. She asked me, *"When would you like to move in?"* I said, *"This weekend, on Friday, to be precise."* She was shocked and wondered why it was so fast. I told her I needed to move out of the company's apartment. She said, *"Okay! You can get the keys earlier and move in as fast as you can."*

I called my husband to tell him the good news. Quickly, I moved out of the company's apartment and asked my husband to bring in my belongings, as I had found a new home. Oma gave me the keys and never required documents like most landlords would from a foreigner. She trusted that she made the right choice with me. She later told me after

I AM MICKY

I moved in that over fifty people had applied for the flat. Again, nature had smiled at me.

Moving Into a New House

Settling into this house marked the best decision I ever made. It had a charming garden, friendly neighbors, and Oma, whose comforting presence filled me with a sense of security. Its proximity to my workplace made it ideal. It truly felt like fate had guided me to the perfect place. Leaving behind **Kassel** initially made me doubt, but **Altenburg** surpassed all expectations. I found everything I needed here—from a reliable hairstylist, considering I always struggled to find one in **Kassel,** to shops stocking African food items. Oma always welcomed me to church events at the **Brüder Kirche Altenburg,** connecting me to a community I hadn't realized I was missing. The natural beauty of **Altenburg** further lifted my spirits. It deepened my gratitude, reminding me to appreciate life's simple pleasures more deeply each day.

Settling Into My Job

As I settled into my job, I noticed a profound change within myself. Each passing day brought a growing sense of healing and happiness. Michaela, my boss, played a significant role in this transformation. She didn't just manage me; she led with love, patience, and kindness. I often wondered if Michaela had undergone special training for her exceptional managerial skills. She encouraged me to share my ideas and always reassured me during moments of anxiety. Her unwavering support and recognition of my abilities boosted my confidence. Whenever I excelled, she ensured I knew about it, showering me with praise and credit. If there were any issues with colleagues, she handled them with grace, always advocating for me. Every morning, I looked forward to seeing her at work. During her absence on holiday, she entrusted me with responsibilities, demonstrating her confidence in me. Michaela healed something within me and also liberated me from past emotional traumas. For her genuine care and support, I am profoundly grateful. *"Thank you, Michaela, for being an exceptional boss, mentor, and friend."* God knew Micky needed a Michaela.

A Change

Michaela was away on holiday, but our communication remained constant. We stayed in touch during her absence, sharing updates about work. Meanwhile, I found myself engaged in the responsibilities of handling quality management activities. Then came the official email from management. I knew something would happen, but I didn't know what exactly. Strangely, I experienced a striking dream two months into the job. In it, I found myself in a different office altogether, surrounded by unfamiliar surroundings. I thought it was a promotion because I was on a different floor. Usually, my office was downstairs at the production unit. Still, in the dream, I saw myself on the top floor of a company. Upon waking up, I wrote about my dream in my journal app, interpreting it as a promotion. However, reality soon dawned on me. Rather than a promotion, it predicted a significant shift in my career, revealing the next chapter in my journey.

We scheduled a meeting with management, which was how I learned what was happening in the company. A financial crisis threatened the closure of one of its branches, and they were informing us about the possibility of losing our jobs. While the possibility of losing my job weighed on my mind, I opted to await Michaela's return before taking action. When she arrived, there was another meeting, and it became clear that our branch was also at risk of closure. The company instructed us to move our activities to the home office in the coming months. During my time at home, I took a casual approach to job hunting, using it to explore new possibilities, discover new places, and refine my interviewing skills.

I couldn't imagine parting ways with Michaela. She was an exceptional boss, and I admired her management style. We planned a get-together in the coming weeks, eagerly anticipating seeing each other after a long absence. As we traveled on the train, I shared with her the details of my job applications and the offers I had received, as I was in demand everywhere I applied. However, I told her, *"I never want to leave Altenburg."*

Remember the house we spotted in the newspaper on our first day in **Altenburg?** We bought it. Three months after moving into a new city, I co-owned my first rental property in **Germany.** *"Acquiring the house was a no-brainer—it was affordable, readily available, and indeed the best decision we could have made."*

The Search

I updated Michaela about the house and told her I was reluctant to leave, having grown fond of **Altenburg.** She said there had been no updates regarding the company's future in the following months. In response, I assured her of my patience, telling her I would wait as I was not hurrying to make decisions. Later that evening, amidst the company of our colleagues, we enjoyed a delightful time together before I departed for home. As I waited, I constantly communicated with God, expressing my earnest desire to remain in my current location. I needed a community here as I had not found a church that held constant services yet. Additionally, I desired a friend who loved God, shared my faith, and could provide support and encouragement during times of temptation and spiritual struggle.

I was on holiday in **Kassel** in December when Michaela called me with disturbing news. She said, *"You may receive a letter stating the company will terminate your contract. Discussions are ongoing as a new company is about to buy the old one."* Despite the tension, she reassured me, *"I believe you'll secure another job. Your qualifications and intelligence speak for themselves."* I acknowledged her words with a simple *"Okay!"*. After my holiday, I returned to **Altenburg,** where I once again prayed to God. Before, I would ask Him, *"Why did you choose Altenburg for me"* but this time, I asked Him something different. I told God, *"You can't bring me here and let me move again. I am not moving."* I reminded Him that I needed a supportive friend and a Christian community, as these were the necessities lacking in **Altenburg.**

Although I received job offers from other companies, they were far from **Altenburg.** Considering my present state, it would have been easy to accept, but I remained determined not to relocate. *"I will continue living in **Altenburg,** come what may."*

An Answered Prayer

Intentionally, I applied to smaller companies around **Altenburg.** Michaela shared companies with me and later recommended me for a quality manager position, only that the company was very far away. I struggled with this decision but decided to do the first interview anyway. I delayed giving my confirmation to the interviewer for the site visit as I knew I didn't want to move yet. Despite Michaela's recommendation and the opportunity, I hesitated due to the distance.

One day, as I casually browsed through **Glassdoor,** a popular recruitment site, I stumbled upon a company I had jokingly applied to a few months back, not expecting much. Surprisingly, despite receiving no response, I noticed a fresh opening for a different role that interested me. Without hesitation, I submitted my application. To my delight, a week later, I received a call from them expressing interest in my CV and extending an invitation for an interview. They were ready to offer me a position in **Quality Management.** Delighted at the opportunity, I accepted and scheduled the interview for the following week.

The interview went well, and afterward, the interviewer encouraged me to provide feedback if I was interested in moving on with the position. Realizing this was my opportunity, I promptly followed up. I received offers from other companies, some even offering higher pay, yet I turned them down. I liked the company I discovered on Glassdoor. While one of the companies was much closer to my home, it didn't align with my standards, encouraging me to decline their offer.

While awaiting a response regarding the next stage, I received a call from another company based in **Altenburg**. Upon arriving for their interview, the behavior of the girl who was to interview me struck me as rude and racist. Due to her manners, I politely excused myself, expressed gratitude, and showed my disinterest in continuing the interview. I told her with faith that I had a job already, which was how I left the premises. After returning home, I called the company I applied with from **Glassdoor,** and we scheduled a **probe day (probation work).** During this period, I would meet Mr. Andy, the company manager. Upon meeting him, I immediately sensed the positive atmosphere of the workplace. Excitedly, upon my return home, I shared the news with my family, including my husband and Oma. Addressing Oma, I proclaimed, *"I told you I'm not going anywhere. I'll secure a job right here."*

I anxiously awaited their official offer and contract, my impatience growing with each moment. In anticipation, I was already forming samples of what my official email would look like. My concern lingered, particularly regarding how my long name would fit with the company's longer name. As time passed, my impatience grew, and I contemplated applying to another company. Just as I was about to take that step, my phone rang—it was the company. *"We're pleased to inform you that we've decided to extend the job offer to you,"* the voice on the other end exclaimed. *"We'll send over the contract shortly, and you're welcome to start on February 1st or at any other time that suits you best."* And just like that, I had secured the job!

Dreams Turning into Reality

Landing my new job was my dream come true. Initially, I thought it was a promotion at my old company. Still, it became apparent that this was my next life phase with a different organization. I resumed the new company, and I noticed a girl always smiling at me during my first two days at the new job. Her name was Natalie. One day, while washing my hands by the sink during a tour, she approached me and said, *"I know you are new, and I am glad you are here."* I thanked her but wondered why she said that.

The following day, we had lunch, discussing specific topics, including her desire to try **African** food. I promised to invite her for some *Nigeria Jollof*—a popular rice dish in Nigeria. She was excited about this. We built our friendship by talking daily in the office while sharing our work activities. Every morning, we would wait for each other before and after finishing work. One day, as we were saying our goodbyes at the office entrance, Natalie mentioned that she had a long drive home, about 30 minutes each way. This prompted me to ask if she listened to music on the way. *"Yes, I do,"* she replied. Curious, I asked about the type of music. *"I play worship songs while I drive,"* she answered. Delighted, I responded, *"I do that too!"* She smiled warmly and said, *"Nice! I am a Christian."* "So am

I," I replied, feeling a bond forming between us. Finding a true youth in **Germany who** was genuine about God was rare. I eagerly asked, *"Could you share your Spotify playlist with me when you get home?"* She happily agreed. Inspired by her music, I crafted my playlist and named it *"Natalie playlist."*

The following week, Natalie visited me for the *Nigerian Jollof rice I had* promised. After dinner, which she particularly enjoyed—Jollof rice with fried chicken and plantain, she commented that it was a great combination. She brought a movie titled ***"The Shack,"*** a Christian-based film about a man who lost his child and struggled with forgiveness. As we watched the film, we spoke and shared our struggles. I told her about my issues with my mother and how I hadn't spoken to her for almost six months. She encouraged me to forgive her and offered to pray with me before leaving. These moments renewed my connection with God. We became friends on the Bible App and started rereading the Bible daily—I had stopped before. Planning to start a Bible reading challenge motivated me to return to my old routine.

I was grateful to God for answering my prayers with a friend like Natalie. After meeting her, my conversations with God became more frequent, and soon, I began to witness His wonders in my life. Each day, as I went to work, I listened to the *"Natalie Playlist,"* which lifted my spirits and helped me reconnect with God through a music habit I had in the past.

Coincidentally, I have struggled with my sleep since starting my new job. I woke up every day at 3 AM, which was strange as I usually enjoy long periods of sleep. I complained to my old dear friend Naomi, and she said, *"Maybe God is trying to tell you something. So, whenever you wake up, pray and ask him what he wants to tell you."* With the renewed Bible reading routine, I heard God speak directly to me from *Ephesians 2:10*, which inspired the writing of this book. I stood up suddenly after reading this verse and started to write my life story. It felt like I was drunk in spirit as I continued this daily writing routine by 3 AM, waking up through the spirit of God.

I AM MICKY

Some weeks later, I received a WhatsApp message from my old boss, Michaela, inquiring if I was enjoying my work, as she had just received an offer from the new company. I assured her that my job was great, that I loved it, and I was having the best time of my life. She was pleased for me, but my happiness originated from more than the job satisfaction—I was happier to remain close to Michaela, my dear Oma, and in **Altenburg,** my favorite city where God had led me to heal and find purpose.

THE END

I AM MICKY

CONCLUSION

I emerged from a broken environment, but I refused to let that hurt dictate the course of my life. I understand too well the struggles many children face today, enduring neglect and shame as they navigate the mess of a rough household. These children need to hear and understand that it is not their fault. Their parents, overwhelmed by their challenges, may not know any better. I am now reconnecting more with my family.

My journey was filled with suffering due to this pain, yet somehow, it also brought about change. The misery I endured became a powerful motivator, pushing me forward with a relentless determination to break the cycle and avoid repeating the same mistakes. Now, my focus has shifted towards extending a guiding hand to other children trapped within the confines of damage. It is a challenging journey that I'm committed to undertaking. Just as I received assistance along my path, particularly from

Jesus, who bore the weight of my burdens when they became too overwhelming to bear alone, I am determined to pay it forward.

With the support of faith and the grace of divine intervention, I've experienced firsthand the life-changing power of relying on a higher being. When I allowed Jesus to step in, I discovered that the weight on my shoulders was reduced, and tasks that once seemed impossible became easier with less effort from me. This realization drives my determination to share this message of hope and assistance with others struggling. Through compassion and faith, I aim to empower others to overcome their hurt and find solace in knowing they are not alone on their journey toward healing and completeness.

My life has been propelled not by my intelligence, cleverness, or strength for almost three decades but by sheer willpower. My unwavering determination for progress and drive for more have kept me moving forward, pushing me to achieve goals and meet deadlines despite any obstacles that stood in my way. Excuses were never part of my vocabulary. Instead, I saw every challenge as an opportunity waiting to be seized. I persisted even when circumstances seemed dire, such as when I had every reason to quit my education. I begged my way through senior secondary school, sacrificed personal possessions like my phone to afford university entrance exams, and acquired skills without the guidance of adults. Do you notice a pattern here? The will to act propels us forward, powered by passion and perseverance rather than mere intelligence. When this will is grounded in faith in God, failure becomes impossible.

I planned to launch this book when I turn 30, but that is not the case now. Due to the intervention of the Holy Spirit and the timely relevance of its message, I decided to release it earlier. If you're reading this book, it could mean any of these: you've obtained an early copy, or divine intervention has prompted an earlier launch, coinciding with my recent twenty-ninth birthday on May 10. Reflecting on this milestone, I feel an overwhelming sense of accomplishment. I finally wrote the book I struggled to articulate until a revelation struck on March 10, 2024, while reading the Bible.

I should have launched my Non-Governmental Organization (NGO) dedicated to fighting domestic violence and providing free education for affected children—a cause to which I've committed my resources, including donating my land in Benin to construct a safe haven. Additionally, plans should be ongoing to establish a community to empower women and men in real estate, cryptocurrency, and stock investment in **Germany.** Collaborations with investors to launch my first **Food Safety App** should also be in progress. Meanwhile, my younger siblings have achieved significant milestones: one graduated as a **Computer Engineer,** and the other as a **Registered Nurse.**

I work in a job I am passionate about, surrounded by colleagues I deeply care for, including Natalie, Swantje, Jean, and Emma. Life couldn't be more fulfilling. While I may not yet be a millionaire, my happiness and contentment are immeasurable. After seven years of isolation, I eagerly anticipate the prospect of seeing my family often.

As I conclude this book, I'm filled with joy. The conciseness of this entry might misrepresent its profound importance to me. The next page will unveil what lies ahead in my journey. While I have many plans, I surrender to the will of my Heavenly Father, acknowledging that His plan surpasses my own.

"When you pass through the waters, I will be with you; and when you pass through the rivers, they will not sweep over you. When you walk through the fire, you will not be burned; the flames will not set you ablaze." Isaiah 43:2 NIV

I AM MICKY

♫ Song for You ♫

I am wonderfully made; I am prayerfully made.

I belong to God; I resemble Him,

I belong to God; I resemble Him.

That's why the devil trembles, trembles,

Whenever he hears me say, "I am God's own,"

The apple of His eye.

QUESTIONS AND ANSWERS

Why launch this book now? Why tell your story?

If you've explored my story, you'd grasp my background. I'm launching this book to financially support my Non-Governmental Organization (NGO) and help those enduring domestic violence. The timing feels right; domestic violence incidents continue to rise, both in Germany and Nigeria. Often overlooked are the children who witness and endure it all in the fallout of their parents. Through divine intervention, I found healing, and now I aim to extend that healing to others through this book. God's persistent hints to me for over three weeks finally made me realize His message: to share my story of His love and protection. He became my father, my confidant, my everything. I completed this book in just one week after receiving this divine message. While the idea to write this book has lingered for some time, it was only with His divine inspiration that I found the motivation to write it. If you're interested, I will share the initial drafts with you.

What is your advice to the world?

I highly recommend getting to know Jesus genuinely and wholeheartedly. A great starting point is the book **"God and the Big Bang."** My book is rooted in faith and belief, so consider sharing it with someone who could benefit from seeing and experiencing Jesus's love.

What is the goal of the NGO?

For a considerable period, I have weighed this question: Micky, what is your goal for this NGO? Having experienced the stress of domestic violence firsthand, I aim to let parents understand the consequences of raising children in environments where violence takes place. Additionally, I want parents to know they can become independent and raise their children safely, even in such situations, by offering scholarships for education and empowering women with financial independence and entrepreneurial skills. Creating awareness about the dangers of domestic violence in the home should be preached and encouraged. This way, individuals will be more concerned about avoiding them.

Where will the profit from the sales of this book go?

I propose allocating 75% of the book's profit to the NGO. This funding would support building a safe haven for men, women, and children in Benin City, Edo State, Nigeria, and provide free scholarships for education and skill acquisition programs. I am also open to partnering with other NGOs and utilizing crowdfunding to address specific needs as they arise. Additionally, as guided by my faith, I intend to contribute a portion of my monthly salary.

I AM MICKY

What's next before age 30?

I plan to continue my career in the job I love, transitioning into auditing within the food industry. However, I don't intend to work indefinitely. Having spent too much time away from my family, I aspire to spend more time with them and devote the remaining portion of my life to my NGO, assisting others through increased volunteering—Helping others has always been my passion, and I've consistently utilized my privileges for this cause.

Pursuing a **PhD** in the future wouldn't be out of the question, as attaining the *"Doctor"* title would be rewarding. I may even enter politics if it aligns with divine guidance. My natural desire to serve others fuels this aspiration, and I would wholeheartedly embrace the opportunity.

Who are your role models?

To be honest, I do not have any, but maybe a few women inspire me: Genevieve Nnaji, Viola Davis,

219

Linda Ikeji, and Ife, the owner of *Dang Lifestyle*. I love these women as they motivate me to be better. To add to the list, I now have a career mentor I look up to for advice.

If you're interested in supporting us, there are several ways you can contribute:

1. **Financial Support**: Your donations help us fund essential programs and initiatives. Please message us on our Facebook and Instagram pages.
2. **Volunteer**: Your time and skills are invaluable to us. Join our team of volunteers and contribute to our mission firsthand. For more information on volunteer opportunities, contact us on Facebook and Instagram @the_mickymarisfoundation.
3. **Spread the Word**: Share my book with your friends, family, and colleagues. Follow us on Facebook and Instagram @the_mickymarisfoundation. Your support, in any form, is crucial to furthering our

mission and positively impacting the lives of those we serve.

Thank you for considering supporting us!

Insights From Friends and Loved Ones: Reflections

In humility, I have chosen to know what people say about me. I sent messages to friends (old and new) and family, asking them to share personal stories and reflections about me. Their thoughts are now on display.

Rita Nwaye (met her in 2018)
Serial Entrepreneur, Abuja, Nigeria.

Micky is my very good friend. When I met her, she was a **BSc holder,** and we met at the International Airport in Abuja. Currently, she has many qualifications. I usually call her my *"Paddy,"* meaning my "*best friend"* in pidgin English. She's fun to be with; you will laugh and have lovely moments anytime she's around. She's a goal-getter and super smart. Micky thinks fast and always has a solution to everyone's problems because of her kind of person.

I AM MICKY

Sharon Itua (an online friend I met in 2022)
Project Manager, MMF, Kaduna, Nigeria.

Micky isn't just full of life—she's a life force. She's resilient, passionate, always ready to lend a hand, and welcomes you with a warm smile. When Micky told me she was writing a book, I knew the world had to experience her infectious enthusiasm and unwavering determination. She's the kind of person who makes you want to be a better version of yourself.

Owa Agbonyinma Naomi (an online friend I met in 2017)
CEO of PLEASANT PALMA Ltd, Edo State, Nigeria.

Micky and I initially connected over an investment opportunity. My schoolmates always mentioned her, earning her the nickname **"The Great Micky."** She's a great friend and feels like a sister to me.

I AM MICKY

Marshia (former schoolmate, Uni Kassel 2019) Stuttgart, Germany.

A Beacon of Support and Joy: My Friend Micky

Micky has been my rock since our university days in Germany. Her care and support have been unwavering through exams and solitary moments. She's a compassionate soul, always ready to lend a hand or offer a listening ear. Micky is more than just supportive; she's a powerhouse of positivity and resilience. Her infectious zest for life brings laughter and joy to every gathering. She taught me the beauty of being authentically myself, showing me that true happiness comes from embracing our unique selves and connecting genuinely with others. In short, Micky is not just a friend but a beacon of light in my life. Her kindness, strength, and infectious spirit have made an indelible mark on my heart. I'm grateful daily to have her by my side, as I cherish the memories we continue to create together.

I AM MICKY

Kelvin Eboh (former student, University of Kassel 2018)

Accountant, Frankfurt.

Micky is an extraordinary individual whose kindness and selflessness illuminate every aspect of her being. She possesses a rare quality of caring deeply for others, often going above and beyond to ensure their happiness and well-being. Whether it's a simple gesture or a grand act of generosity, Micky consistently demonstrates her unwavering dedication to making those around her feel loved and valued. Her heart is a wellspring of compassion and an innate desire to spread joy and positivity wherever she goes. In a world that can sometimes seem harsh and indifferent, Micky stands out as a beacon of goodness, reminding us of the beauty of genuine kindness. She embodies that the world is better with someone like her 🫶 😊.

I AM MICKY

Chinalu Mbakwe (Friend since 2016)
Life Coach, Lagos, Nigeria.

Micky is an exceptional person who is very determined. She sets a goal and stops at nothing until she achieves that goal. Micky is both resilient and self-aware. She is constantly working on and improving herself, which is evident in everything she does. When Micky told me she wrote a book, I was impressed because I knew she was a great storyteller. I knew she outdid herself this time by taking it up a notch higher. I can't wait for it to be published. I'm sure it will be an enjoyable read.

Dammy Isikalu (met through a mutual friend in 2018)
Real Estate Agent, Abuja, Nigeria.

Micky is enthusiastic, fun to be with, and a goal-getter. One day, I remember us talking about what to do after youth service, and she started bringing up ideas (good ones and funny ones). I love the fact that she never gives up! Once she sets her mind on something, she ensures she gets it, which inspires me greatly. Micky is a soft-hearted person. I see her as someone who hardly gets annoyed. Even if she does, *"I'm sorry"* can fix it, with her forgiving and letting go almost immediately. Micky is always a big vibe! She is fun to be with and always cracks me up. She knows how to light up a dull room, even with her tiny voice. She can never learn to pronounce someone's name correctly; she always hilariously mispronounces names. Micky can be so caring and thoughtful; she knows how to give good advice! I love her so much; I know it's me and her till eternity.

Joyce and Jemie Obadiaru (Siblings)
Registered Nurse - CEO, Jaylit Fashion House |
Tech Experts

Micky is our beloved sister, and we are thrilled to write about her. Words fail to capture her true essence because she is truly extraordinary. She embodies love, peace, compassion, and forgiveness. Micky's kindness towards others and her willingness to help those in need are truly remarkable. She selflessly gives her all to bring happiness and comfort to others. Micky is not just someone who wants to make a positive impact on everyone around her but also the world as a whole. If someone were to say that angels don't exist, I would proudly point to our sister as living proof that they do.

Rene Frank Hermann Schneider (Husband)
International Project Manager, Intercultural coach

An angel lived without a childhood in a world of corruption and poverty. Despite the hardships that surrounded her, she radiated beauty and maturity far beyond her years. Born into a life where survival was a daily battle, she learned the harsh realities of the world early on, yet she never allowed despair to consume her spirit. Instead, she resolved to overcome every obstacle in her path. Many people depict heroes as towering figures of strength and power, akin to Arnold Schwarzenegger. However, for me, a hero embodies something far more profound. It's someone who selflessly cares for others, extends a helping hand in times of need, and embodies kindness and compassion in every action. There's poignant wisdom in the notion that we are all angels with only one wing, yet when we come together, we can soar. Guided by faith and united by love, we find strength in each other's presence. This unity enables us to support, uplift, and inspire one another, paving the way for a brighter future.

Pastor Steve Ogedegbe
Pastor, Artist, and Author (Naked)

Micky turned to her faith for solace in the darkest moments of her life—when all seemed lost, and hope was but a flicker in the distance. Seeking refuge in the church's walls, guidance, and comfort, she poured out her heart in prayer. Though the answers she sought didn't come in the form of immediate relief or miraculous solutions, Micky clung to her unwavering confidence in God. The absence of instant remedies did not shake her faith but strengthened her resolve to persevere through the trials. With each passing day, as she faced the challenges that threatened to consume her, Micky found herself drawing strength from her faith. It was a beacon of hope amid despair, a steadfast anchor in the turbulent seas of uncertainty. Through the trials and tribulations, Micky remained steadfast in her belief that God had a plan for her, even when the path seemed obscured by darkness. And though the road to stability was fraught with obstacles, her faith never wavered. Ultimately, her unwavering confidence in God sustained her through the storm and guided her to a place of stability and peace. Looking back on her journey, Micky knows that her faith carried her through the darkest times and into the light of a new day.

10 TIPS OF LIFE

YOU MIGHT BE curious about what insights a 29-year-old woman could offer about life. Despite any reservations, I have a few pointers that might prove helpful to you. These insights are drawn from the wealth of experiences and knowledge I've acquired.

Life often imparts lessons early, pushing us to grow faster and confront challenges beyond our age. I've encountered individuals I never wished to emulate and situations I hoped never to face. Yet, through these experiences, I've gathered insights that may benefit you.

1. Find Jesus

"Call to Me, and I will answer you, and tell you [and even show you] great and mighty things, [things which have been confined and hidden], which you do not know and understand." NIV Jeremiah 33:3.

I AM MICKY

Throughout my life, I've been a regular attendee of church services, as my mother's devotion to God greatly influenced me. We never missed a Bible study or choir practice. At age 11, I experienced water baptism and actively participated in church activities such as Bible quizzes, gospel role plays, and singing in the choir. Looking back, I vividly remember when I got lost inside the church; these memories reflect my upbringing as a dedicated church girl.

I continued attending church during my university years, although my relationship with Jesus was shallow. He knew me, but I honestly didn't know Him. However, my life took on a new meaning when I finally established a personal relationship with Jesus. I began recognizing His guidance through destiny helpers, angels, and subtle reminders of His grace along my path. As you explore this book, you'll witness instances where Jesus took control of my life, even when I was unaware of His presence, lacked a consistent daily connection with Him, and His work for my benefit wasn't immediately apparent.

Once you discover Him, let Him become the foundation of your life. Allow Him to guide every decision you make, involving Him in everything—from selecting a partner, a home, or a job to forming friendships with people. We are saved by grace, and I strongly advise you to seek out Jesus.

Book Recommendations: The Bible, The Mind and Words of Jesus by J.R. Macduff**, God and the Big Bang** by Daniel C. Matt

2. Write It Down

I deliberately included photos and all my documentation to illustrate the movements, provide evidence, and establish timelines. In December 2019, I had the chance to view a documentary titled **"The Secret,"** which my husband recommended. Before this, I had experimented with writing things down since the age of 14, but I hadn't consistently maintained this habit. However, after watching that documentary, my husband encouraged me to continue with my writing behavior. He said, *"For the* *last 18 years of my life, I wrote down all my visions and achieved them quickly".*

So, grab a pen and paper and jot down your 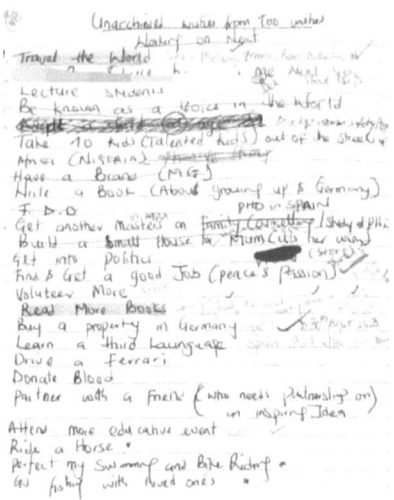 dreams. I agreed with my husband's suggestion: Write it down, believe in it, and live as if it's already yours. This is visualizing how you want things to unfold.

I pulled out a book and wrote down 100 amazing things I aspire to achieve. *Learning to eat salad and writing a book was part of them.*

While a widespread belief in a **Harvard University** study indicates that those who document their goals have higher success rates, my research revealed that **Harvard** did not conduct this study.

Instead, *Gail Matthews (2007)* conducted this study at the **University of Dominican.**

Nevertheless, the study offers proof of the usefulness of three coaching tools: Accountability, Commitment, and the Act of Writing Down One's Goals. So, there you have it—putting things on paper enhances your chances of accomplishing them. That's my reality.

Book Recommendations: Master Key System by Charles Hannel, **The Secret to the Law of Attraction** by Rhonda Byrne, and **Happiness and How to Find It and Keep It** by Joan Duncan Oliver.

3. Avoid Comparison

One practice I always held dear was refraining from comparing myself to others. Whenever I noticed someone achieving success, I celebrated and cheered them on for their accomplishments while expressing gratitude to the higher powers. I believe comparisons corrupt a part of one's self; they steal away joy. Yet, despite our best efforts, the urge to compare can sometimes sneak in. However, we can defeat this tendency by cultivating gratitude and embracing our uniqueness and talents.

Say, *"I am unique and have a gift no one else has, and I would bless others with this gift."*

I am about 5.2 feet tall—yes, it's on the shorter side, but it's all good! Despite my height, I take pride in being the funniest and sweetest person you'll ever encounter. Being around me brings joy and positive energy, and chatting with me will surely lift your spirits. That is who I am, and I consider myself fortunate not to tower over others in height.

4. Do Not Fear

I understand that facing fear is challenging. It's a feeling that can grip us, often manifesting as a knot in the pit of our stomachs. Despite experiencing this emotion, I refuse to let it dictate my actions. If you explore my story, you'll find instances where fear crept into the background, threatening to hold me back. Yet, I pressed forward, refusing to allow fear to reign supreme.

Fear has been a constant companion throughout my journey, attempting to discourage me from pursuing my dreams and ambitions. But rather than surrendering to its grip, I've confronted it head-on. Despite the challenges and uncertainty fear brings, I've consistently summoned the courage to take bold steps.

Even in the face of intimidating odds, I've refused to let fear paralyze me. I've embraced the discomfort, recognizing that growth often lies beyond our comfort zones. By pushing past my fears, I've uncovered new opportunities, developed meaningful connections, and achieved personal milestones that I once believed were out of my reach.

So, while fear may linger, threatening to undermine our resolve, we must remember that we possess the power to overcome it. By accepting and confronting our fears with courage and determination, we can navigate life's challenges and pursue our aspirations with unwavering conviction.

You can do it too.

Do it scared

Do it with the feeling in your belly

Just Do It (Nike).

5. Smile

Ah, I can see that beautiful smile on your face—it suits you perfectly. A smile is the finest attire you can wear, don't you agree? Many people recognize me as a constantly cheerful individual. I enjoy laughter and smiling, even in the face of adversity. Indeed, I often crack jokes during challenging times, which might lead some people to believe I am strange. But those smiles are my lifeline—they infuse me with hope and help keep my mind steady amidst the chaos.

Smiling isn't just a reflex; it's a powerful tool that calms the mind and eases tension. When we smile, our brains receive signals of reassurance, reminding us to stay cheerful in the face of difficulties. So, let that smile brighten your day and spread joy to those around you. After all, *a smile is the most beautiful accessory you can ever wear.*

6. Minimize

As someone who embraces a simple lifestyle, I've learned that it saves money and helps me avoid unnecessary decision-making. People have questioned why I didn't wear a diamond wedding ring in the past, and my response is always simple: it's not essential to me. While my husband can afford it, I focus on practicality over extravagance. I only purchase items I love but do so in the most economical manner possible.

Let me share a game-changing approach to spending wisely. If the concept of smart spending doesn't resonate with you, you may skip this page, but I strongly advise against it. Always know that obtaining high value for a lower cost is possible—I speak from experience. While I own designer items, I've never paid outrageous prices for them. Instead, I've capitalized on the overproduction common in fashion and other industries, acquiring quality goods without breaking the bank. You can do the same! Here are a few strategies.

I. **Buy Pre-Owned:** Offer to buy items from people who originally paid top dollar. Often, they are willing to sell at a fraction of the original price. These opportunities are usually found in flea markets.

II. **Seasonal Sales:** Wait for a change in season. Last season's items often go on sale to make room for new inventory, providing an opportunity to buy quality goods at reduced prices. Buy summer stuff short before winter begins, and vice versa.

III.   **Massive Sales:** Look for major sales events. These are great ways to score designer items at a significant discount.

NOTE: You can enjoy luxury items without the price tag by being patient and strategic.

I've firmly been against wasteful behavior in all its forms—food, money, or resources. My mother instilled this mindset in me long before introducing the **Sustainable Development Goals (SDGs). SDG 12,** which focuses on responsible consumption and production, highlights the importance of reducing waste and embracing sustainability. The **second-hand market** serves as a testament to the practicality of this approach.

While pursuing my Master's at the **University of Kassel/Fulda (Witzenhausen campus),** sustaina-bility was a core principle of our values. Lecturers and peers were committed to living in a manner that reduced environmental impact and avoided wasteful practices. In a world where **carbon dioxide**

(CO2) levels are skyrocketing, we must become part of the solution rather than add to the problem.

One piece of advice I hold dear is, "N*ever purchase a new car unless I have a compelling business reason to do so and stand to benefit from tax incentives.*" The depreciation of a new car begins the moment you drive it off the lot. Take, for example, my first car—a **Renault Clio.** We acquired it for two thousand five hundred (2,500) euros, which was a relatively modest sum, and after driving it for a short period, I sold it for a profit despite the increase in mileage. Rene shared this lesson with me about **smart vehicle purchasing. In Germany,** I've sharpened my skills in selling used cars while consistently turning every transaction into profits. Buying and selling second-hand vehicles has proven to be a lucrative strategy for minimizing expenses and increasing savings.

Lastly, understanding the difference between **needs** and **wants** is paramount in making informed purchasing decisions. Through a business course at the **University of Benin,** I gained clarity on this topic for the first time. A **need is something essential, something you can't do without,** whereas a **want** is **something you could live without.** For instance, while I need to eat healthy, organic food for my well-being, I want a Porsche Cayenne. Recognizing this difference has enabled me to prioritize my spending effectively—I drive a smart car, which fulfills my transportation needs without unnecessary extravagance.

7. Have A Side Hustle

Having a side hustle has been a vital part of my life journey, starting from my early teenage years. At 16, I ventured into my first entrepreneurial career by selling old, used Blackberry phones at the university. This experience taught me a valuable lesson: **Find items that people are willing to sell cheaply, improve their value through repairs or refurbishment, and then sell them for a profit.** This simple yet effective formula became the cornerstone of my side hustle ventures.

During the early days of my marriage to Rene, we experienced financial struggles due to debt. Determined to overcome this challenge, we turned to the **flea market scene** to generate additional income. Every weekend, we would rise at dawn, load our truck with carefully selected items sourced from **flea markets** and **garage sales,** and head to our destinations: **flea markets** in **Kassel (Messe), Kassel (Metro),** or wherever we could set up our stand.

Together, we transformed our booth into a visually appealing showcase, carefully arranging our goods to captivate potential buyers. We understood the importance of standing out in a crowded marketplace. So, we dressed well, exuding professionalism and warmth. While I managed the stand, Rene embarked on scouting missions, utilizing his sharp negotiating skills to procure high-value items at bargain prices from neighboring stands and sell them for double the price. He applied this intelligent approach to **real estate transactions,** demonstrating his entrepreneurial sense in various arenas.

Our flea market ventures were just one aspect of our diverse side hustle—another lucrative endeavor involved selling **antique gems on eBay.** We leveraged our keen eye for valuable flea market finds and turned them into profitable online sales. We sharpened our entrepreneurial skills with each transaction and expanded our financial horizons.

Amidst the hustle and bustle of the **flea market circuit,** I had the pleasure of forging a lasting friendship with Karty, a fellow entrepreneur. Our bond was rooted in shared experiences and mutual respect, enduring the test of time and serving as a testament to the enduring connections forged in pursuing entrepreneurial success.

Resilience, resourcefulness, and a relentless determination to create opportunities for financial prosperity characterized our side hustle journey. Through relentless effort and a commitment to continuous growth, we've transformed our entrepreneurial dreams into concrete realities, one sale at a time.

8. Investing (Assets)

"Invest in seven ventures, yes, in eight; you do not know what disaster may come upon the land." NIV Ecclesiastes 11:2.

I have read many books, and it's a privilege to be married to someone with expertise in asset acquisition. Through our partnership, I've gained significant knowledge about **investing and asset discovery.** One of the standout books that has greatly influenced my understanding of wealth accumulation is **"Rich Dad, Poor Dad"** by *Robert T. Kiyosaki.* Let me share a few key lessons from the book that resonated with me and transformed my approach to money.

- Never work for money. Work for the fun of it, for the connections and relationships you build. I am not saying you should work for free.

- Educate yourself about finance and money by reading good books.

- Identify real assets and invest in them. Please don't buy a house with a 30-year mortgage only to live in it.

- Keep your day job and minimize your expenses. Have a solid side hustle. Don't quit your job. I still work and live on a reasonable budget while my side hustles remain intact.

- Making money takes guts. Take reasonable risks that will yield profits. Read, research, and ask questions.

- Like the rich, you should know the tax system inside out. The government is wise, and you should be wiser.

- Leave specific tasks to professionals. Learn broadly. I have a wide range of knowledge in various areas. Even though I work in **Quality Management,** I can still perform jobs in other departments.

I began investing at 19, and by the time I turned 20, I had already acquired my first piece of landed property. My investment portfolio spans various sectors, including **real estate (rentals), stocks, bonds, ETFs, and cryptocurrencies.** It's important to acknowledge that each investment avenue comes with risks, and it's crucial to assess and manage these risks carefully to make informed decisions.

Additionally, I recommend reading **"The Courage to Be Rich"** by *Suze Orman.* This book explores the mindset and strategies necessary to achieve financial success and security, offering valuable insights that can empower you to take control of your financial future.

9. Choose Independence

Financial freedom protects against many stresses and potential embarrassments for both men and women. Money empowers you with choices and comfort, offering a sense of security that can ease many anxieties in life. *"While it's true that money alone may not guarantee happiness, it provides a sense of security and peace."*

Being the spouse of a wealthy individual, whether it's *Oga's wife (a rich man's wife) or the wife of a famous figure,* may offer certain privileges. Still, there's an outstanding value in being **financially self-sufficient.** Whether married to a *billionaire* or a *king,* having your source of income ensures you carve your path and maintain a sense of freedom.

Despite facing numerous challenges during my university days, including financial limitations, I pursued my education. I recognized that education is vital to opening various possibilities and unlocking doors that may have remained closed.

Choosing not to settle for a lifetime of unskilled labor, such as cleaning houses, doesn't reduce the value of such work but reflects a desire for personal fulfillment and advancement. Over time, I came to understand that many women endure abusive relationships or stay trapped in unhappy situations due to **financial dependency.** The ability to support oneself and provide for one's children often becomes a driving force for women seeking to secure their future and break free from oppressive circumstances.

Pursuing a career or engaging in activities that align with your passions and interests is essential. By earnestly investing in jobs that bring you fulfillment, you not only cultivate personal satisfaction but also have the opportunity to generate income and achieve financial independence. Empower yourself to seize control of your destiny and create a future defined by your aspirations and accomplishments.

Looking back at my journey, I realize that my determination and self-assurance pushed me into the workforce at 15. Throughout my life, I've maintained steadfast confidence, which has opened doors and opportunities for me.

10. Land Yourself a Job

Moments when my confidence spoke volumes have shaped my career revolution. For instance, my second job opportunity occurred without even requiring an interview. Also, my impressive performance during an internship led to managing a new branch—a responsibility bestowed upon me due to my demonstrated capability and confidence.

Even during my national service, where the Manager determined the job placement through a paper game of *"pick yes or no,"* I confidently approached the process, securing a position through my persistent belief in myself.

For over two years in Germany, I worked in the unskilled job sector, including cleaning. Despite my dislike for the work conditions, I approached each task with a smile and cheerful behavior. Remarkably, the company's owners still remember me fondly to date, attesting to the lasting impression I left behind.

Lastly, I remained committed and dedicated during a year of volunteering at **Lebensqualität e.V NGO (Lequa)** at the test center for COVID-19. I was very friendly to the customers and my colleagues. I worked once or twice with the boss, Mr. Steven Renner; he was always impressed with my behavior, which led to him offering me a job afterward. Although the work didn't align with my passions, I tackled it confidently, recognizing the value of gaining experience. I am still a member of the NGO to this day. They focus on helping people with disabilities in everyday life and providing solutions to people with disabilities in **Hessen, Germany.**

Drawing from my wealth of experiences and the confidence that has pushed me forward, let's examine some valuable tips for learning and excelling in any job.

I. **Curriculum Vitae**: Crafting a compelling **curriculum vitae (CV)** is essential. It serves as your first pitch, showcasing your qualifications and experiences even before you can sell yourself in person to your employer. Approach the creation of your CV with care and attention, ensuring that you tailor it to fit the job description you are applying for while using **relevant keywords** that catch your potential employers' attention.

Once your CV effectively sells your abilities, you'll likely progress to the interview stage. Here, the focus shifts from merely presenting your educational background to showcasing your personality and interpersonal skills. Remember, people prefer to collaborate with individuals they like and can connect with on a personal level.

View interviews as **discussions** rather than **interrogations.** Take the opportunity to ask questions, share stories, and inject humor where necessary. Maintain confidence by making eye contact with your interviewer, offering a firm handshake, and seizing every opportunity to advocate for yourself passionately and productively. Approaching interviews with authenticity, warmth, and confidence can significantly enhance your chances of leaving a lasting impression on the interviewer and securing the position you desire. So, be prepared to sell your qualifications, unique personality, and suitability for the role.

II.   **Negotiation:** My experience in Germany began my professional career journey. I quickly learned that negotiation strategies vary based on vital factors such as experience, location, gender, and qualifications. These elements can be practical tools to secure a better **compensation package** for yourself. It's essential not to shy away from discussing money during negotiations; thorough research and understanding of your worth are paramount.

While it's common for companies not to mention salary during the initial interview stage, candidates should prepare to discuss their salary expectations when the conversation arises. I remember the advice I received from my friend Joseph. He said, *"Say a number you can defend during negotiation."*

When you can mention a number, do it confidently based on your skills and market research. During your first job, **prioritize gaining experience and building your professional portfolio over salary.** However, as you progress in your career, **capitalize on your gathered experience as bargaining power to negotiate a more favorable salary**. By strategically utilizing your expertise, you can ensure that your compensation aligns with your contributions and aspirations.

III. **Make a Good First Impression:** In Germany, it's common for candidates to be invited for a **probationary period** following their initial interview. This period presents another valuable opportunity for you to make a positive impression. Take time to connect with people, observe the company culture, and adapt accordingly to demonstrate your suitability for the role.

I highly recommend exploring resources like *Brendan Kane's* book **"Hook Point"** to refine your communication skills further and enhance your ability to engage effectively with others during this crucial phase. By capitalizing on such insights, you can maximize your chances of leaving a lasting and favorable impression on others, setting yourself up for success as you navigate the **probationary period** and beyond.

IV. **Contract:** Congratulations! You've made it to this stage by completing the application process and receiving an offer. However, before you eagerly sign any contracts, take the time to read through the document thoroughly. It's crucial not to rush into agreements blindly.

Pay close attention to those red flags if you need clarification or have concerns. Trust your instincts, and don't hesitate to decline the offer if the warning signs become too obvious. I've personally turned down offers from multiple companies, and I always sense their surprise when I do. Remember, you're not just giving your time and effort to a company; you're offering them value. Ensuring your chosen company truly appreciates and recognizes your worth is essential.

In situations where the answer is no, it's often the better choice in the long run. Feel free to prioritize your well-being and your future.

I AM MICKY

Thank you for attending my TED talk.

Have you enjoyed what you've read? Join my online community for more inspiring content and updates. Follow me on Twitter and TikTok **@I_amMickytaylor** and Instagram **@iam_mickytaylor** to stay connected and be part of my journey.

I AM MICKY

ACKNOWLEDGMENT

First and foremost, I express my heartfelt gratitude to the Holy Spirit, whose unwavering guidance was indispensable in comprehending the task. Without His divine intervention, this book would not have come to fruition.

Natalie, your presence in my life feels heaven-sent, and I am profoundly thankful for allowing God to work through you to aid me on this journey.

To my beloved husband, your unwavering support, love, and care have been my rock. I cherish you deeply.

Kelvin Eboh, you are not just a friend but a cherished brother. Your friendship has been a source of immense strength.

To Pastor Steve Ogedegbe and Mrs. Augusta Ogedegbe, your guidance and nurturing presence in my life, especially during my time in Kassel, are beyond measure. I owe you an immeasurable debt of gratitude.

Joseph and Emelda, your candid conversations on various aspects of life have been invaluable. I hold you both dear to my heart.

Michaela, you were not only my first boss but also an exceptional mentor. Your wisdom and guidance have profoundly shaped my career.

Swantje, your abundant smiles have lightened many of my days. And Jean, your remarkable presence has been a joy.

To my new boss, your humor has brought much-needed levity to our interactions, and I sincerely appreciate it.

A heartfelt thank you goes out to my Godsent editor, Mrs. Chinwendu Ezera Emereze; collaborating with you has been a delight.

I AM MICKY

Naomi, Dammy, and Jumai, you are more than friends; you are family. I am endlessly grateful for your presence in my life.

To Emma, thank you for being an amazing soul. I sincerely appreciate your unwavering support and kindness towards me.

I appreciate my brilliant Project Manager, Sharon Itua, who skillfully oversees my endeavors.

Last but certainly not least, to my siblings, Jemie Obadiaru and Joyce Obadiaru, and my mother, Edith Obadiaru: You are the treasures of my life. I love and cherish each one of you dearly.

May God's blessings be upon you all.

VALUABLE RESOURCES

Zondervan. *The Holy Bible: New International Version, Containing the Old Testament and the New Testament.* Zondervan Bible Publishers, 1996.

Matthews, Gail. *Dominican Scholar Dominican Scholar the Impact of Commitment, Accountability, and Written Goals on the Impact of Commitment, Accountability, and Written Goals on Goal Achievement Goal Achievement.* 2007, scholar.dominican.edu/cgi/viewcontent.cgi?article=1002&context=psychology-faculty-conference-presentations.

Vu, Nicole L., et al. "Children's Exposure to Intimate Partner Violence: A Meta-Analysis of Longitudinal Associations with Child Adjustment Problems." *Clinical Psychology*

Review, vol. 46, June 2016, pp. 25–33,
https://doi.org/10.1016/j.cpr.2016.04.003.

Welle, Deutsche. "Germany Sees Sharp Rise in
Domestic Abuse Cases – DW –
07/11/2023." *Dw.com*, 15 Apr. 2003,
www.dw.com/en/germany-sees-sharp-rise-
in-domestic-abuse-cases/a-66187939.
Accessed 21 Apr. 2024.